1 All about me

A Foundation exercises

Memory check: Countries and nationalities

1 Match the countries with the nationalities.

1	the United States	a	British
2	Italy	b	Argentinian
3	Spain	c	Turkish
4	Portugal	d	Australian
5	Brazil	e	Brazilian
6	China	f	Chinese
7	Britain	g	Italian
8	Greece	h	South African
9	Australia	i	German
10	South Africa	j	Spanish
11	Turkey	k	Greek
12	India	l	Indian
13	Argentina	m	Portuguese
14	Germany	n	American
15	Ireland	o	Irish

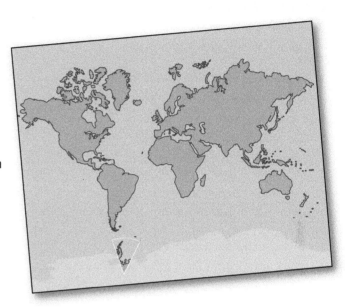

Grammar: Present simple

2 Complete the tables.

+	
I like	music.
She [1] _likes_	football.

−	
I don't like	rugby.
She [2] .... like	tennis.

?	
Do you like basketball?	Yes, I do./No, I [3] ....
[4] .... she like pop music?	Yes, she [5] ..../No, she doesn't.

3 Complete the dialogues with *what* or *where*.

1 **A:** .....*What*..... does Luke want to do?
   B: He wants to play tennis.
2 **A:** .... does your best friend come from?
   B: She comes from Italy.
3 **A:** .... do you go to school?
   B: I go to school in Brighton.
4 **A:** .... kind of music do your parents like?
   B: They like rock music.
5 **A:** .... does Seb want to be?
   B: He wants to be a professional footballer.

About you

4 Answer the questions about you.

1 Do you like music?
   Yes, I do./No, I don't ....
2 Does your dad/mum like football?
   ....
3 Do you play football?
   ....
4 Does your dad/mum play tennis?
   ....
5 Do you live in a small house?
   ....

A Activation exercises

Memory check: Countries and nationalities

1 Complete the crossword.

Across

3   Juan comes from Spain. He's ..... .
5   Bruce comes from Australia. He's ..... .
8   Maria comes from Portugal. She's ..... .
9   Oliver is British. He comes from ..... .
10 Maggie is Irish. She comes from ..... .

Down

1   Hanna is German. She comes from ..... .
2   Apala is Indian. She comes from ..... .
4   Lian comes from China. She's ..... .
6   Giovanni comes from Italy. He's ..... .
7   Omar is Turkish. He comes from ..... .

| 3 S | P | A | N | I | S | H |

Grammar: Present simple

2 Choose the correct words.

Hi, I'm Sophie and I ¹*live* / *lives* in England. My friend Seb also ²*live* / *lives* in England but his mum and dad ³*come* / *comes* from Brazil. What about you? Where ⁴*you live* / *do you live*?

Hi, I'm Luke. I'm South African but I ⁵*don't* / *doesn't* live in South Africa. My family and I ⁶*live* / *lives* in the UK. My friend Gary ⁷*don't* / *doesn't* live in the UK. He's Australian. He ⁸*email* / *emails* me every week. Where does your best friend ⁹*live* / *lives*?

3 Complete the email with the correct verb forms. Use the present simple.

Hi Jack,

My family and I ¹ ___live___ (live) in Manchester, in the UK, but we ² .... (come) from Australia. I ³ .... (play) tennis at school but I ⁴ .... (not like) it. My brother ⁵ .... (like) it and he ⁶ .... (play) every day. I ⁷ .... (love) music and I ⁸ .... (want) to be a pop star one day. My brother ⁹ .... (not want) to be a pop star. He ¹⁰ .... (want) to be a professional tennis player!

Write to me about you and your family.

Mickey

4 Write the words in the correct order.

1 do come you from? where

Where do you come from?

2 friend does your where live?

....

3 what to be? you want do

....

4 of what kind do like? music you

....

5 do play? you what sports

....

6 grandparents where your from? do come

....

5 Match the questions in Exercise 4 with these answers. There are two extra answers.

a I want to be a teacher.   ....

b No, we don't.   ....

c I come from Spain.   *1*

d I like rock music.   ....

e She lives in London.   ....

f I play tennis and basketball.   ....

g They come from Italy.   ....

h Yes, she does.   ....

6 Complete the dialogue with the correct form of *live*, *like* or *want*.

Sophie: Who are the people in the photo, Luke?

Luke: They're my friends, Joyce and Lundi.

Sophie: Are they South African?

Luke: Yes, they are, but they ¹ *don't live* in South Africa.

Sophie: Where ² .... they ....?

Luke: Joyce ³ .... in New Zealand and Lundi ⁴ .... in the United States.

Sophie: ⁵ .... they .... music?

Luke: Yes, they ⁶ .... it very much. Lundi ⁷ .... to be a pop star.

Sophie: What ⁸ .... Joyce .... to be?

Luke: Well, she ⁹ .... to be a pop star. She ¹⁰ .... to be a professional footballer.

English today

7 Match the sentences with the speech bubbles.

a I'm an awesome player!

b That's nice of you, Mark.

c What do you mean?

d Where do you come from, Nick?

3

A Extension exercises

1 Write sentences about the pictures.

Sarah

1 (come from) *She comes from the UK.*
2 (play) ....
3 (like) ....
4 (want to be) ....

Batista   Emilio

5 (live)   *They live in Brazil.*
6 (play)   ....
7 (like)   ....
8 (want to be) ....

2 Complete the dialogue. Write one or two words in each gap.

Sarah: Hi, Batista. Where are you from?

Batista: Brazil. I come ¹ ..... *from* ..... Rio de Janeiro but I ² .... live there.

Sarah: ³ .... do you live?

Batista: I live in Brasilia.

Sarah: Do you like it there?

Batista: Yes, I ⁴ .... But my friend Emilio ⁵ .... like it. He wants ⁶ .... live in Rio!

Sarah: ⁷ .... sports do you play?

Batista: I play football and basketball.

Sarah: ⁸ .... you want to be: a professional footballer or basketball player?

Batista: A professional basketball player. ⁹ .... love sports!

About you

3 Write about you. Use these words.

come from	like	live	play	want to be

My name is Petros and I'm Greek. I come from …

My name ....
....
....
....
....
....
....
....
....
....
....
....
....
....
....

B Foundation exercises

Vocabulary: Daily activities

1 Complete the words.

1 do homework

2 wr_t_ _m__ls

3 l_st_n to m_s_c

4 r_d_ a b_ke

5 m_k_ m_d_l __r_pl_n_s

6 w_lk the d_g

7 w_tch TV

8 c__k br__kf_st

9 sk_t_b__rd

Grammar: Present continuous; Present continuous and present simple

2 Choose the correct words. Then match the sentences with the pictures in Exercise 1.

a You *am / are / is* writing emails. ⟶ _2_

b She *am / are / is* cooking breakfast. ⟶ ....

c I *am / are / is* watching TV. ⟶ ....

d They *am / are / is* skateboarding. ⟶ ....

e He *am / are / is* riding his bike. ⟶ ....

f We *am / are / is* listening to music. ⟶ ....

g You *am / are / is* doing your homework. ⟶ ....

h He *am / are / is* walking the dog. ⟶ ....

i They *am / are / is* making model aeroplanes. ⟶ ....

About you

3 Answer the questions about you.

1 Are you sitting in your room at the moment?
   Yes, I am./No, I'm not.

2 Do you watch TV every evening?

....

3 Is your dad/mum cooking at the moment?

....

4 Does your best friend write poems?

....

5 Do you often play computer games?

....

6 Are you listening to music at the moment?

....

B Activation exercises

Vocabulary: Daily activities

1 Match the sentence halves. Use the pictures to help you.

1 She's surfing
2 They're riding
3 He's walking
4 They're playing
5 She's cooking
6 They're making
7 She's
8 He's doing
9 They're listening
10 She's watching

a his homework.
b to music.
c a model aeroplane.
d skateboarding.
e TV.
f the Internet.
g their bikes.
h computer games.
i breakfast.
j his dog.

Grammar: Present continuous; Present continuous and present simple

2 Complete the text with the correct verb forms.

dance	do	listen	play	ride	surf	walk	~~write~~

Saturday 10th May: What the family is doing!

The weather today is awful, so I'm at home.
I'm ^{1} _writing_ emails to all my friends.
Mum is ^{2} _____ the Internet. Emma is
in her room but she isn't ^{3} _____ her
homework. She's ^{4} _____ to music. What
a surprise! And my dad is ^{5} _____ to
the music (No, please don't, Dad!). My friend
Seb isn't here. He's ^{6} _____ football in
the park with his friends.

I can see some people outside. One man
is ^{7} _____ his dog and two kids are
^{8} _____ their bikes – in the rain!
Saturdays are boring! ☹

Now my cousin Sophie is here. We're playing
computer games. Saturdays are OK! ☺

Luke

3 **Choose the correct words.**

1 Seb often (plays) / is playing computer games on Saturdays but today he chats / (is chatting) to a friend online.

2 Sophie walks / is walking the dog every afternoon. Today she walks / is walking him in the park.

3 Luke often chats / is chatting with his friends online but he doesn't chat / isn't chatting with them now.

4 Emma and her dad watch / are watching football on TV. They always watch / are watching their favourite team.

5 I don't do / am not doing my homework in the evenings. I do / am doing it in the afternoons.

6 Dad cooks / is cooking breakfast at the moment. He always cooks / is cooking on Sundays.

4 **Complete the questions. Then look at the table and write answers.**

On Friday afternoons ...

	Charlie	Sue	Jack	Olivia
at the moment	chat online	skateboard	surf the Internet	skateboard
usually	play football	do homework	cook for his family	do homework

1 A: *Is Charlie chatting* .... (Charlie / chat) online at the moment?
B: *Yes, he is.*

2 A: .... (Charlie / usually / play) football?
B: ....

3 A: .... (Sue and Olivia / skateboard) at the moment?
B: ....

4 A: .... (Sue and Olivia / usually / do) their homework?
B: ....

5 A: .... (Jack / play) football at the moment?
B: ....

6 A: .... (Jack / usually / surf) the Internet?
B: ....

7 A: .... (Sue / skateboard) at the moment?
B: ....

8 A: .... (Jack / usually / cook) for his family?
B: ....

5 **Complete the sentences.**

★★★★ = always   ★★★ = usually   ★★ = often   ★ = sometimes   ☆ = never

1 I *always* play computer games with my friends after school. (★★★★)
2 My mum .... cooks dinner. My dad cooks it. (☆)
3 My best friend .... writes poems and songs. (★★)
4 My sister and I .... watch football on TV on Sunday afternoons. (★★★)
5 My parents .... ride their bikes in the park. (★)
6 I .... cook breakfast for my family on Saturdays. (★★)
7 You .... walk the dog after school. (★★★★)
8 My cousins .... write emails in the evenings. (★★★)

About you

6 **Write about six things you do or don't do.**

1 .... (★★★★)
2 .... (★★★)
3 .... (★★)
4 .... (★)
5 .... (☆)
6 .... (☆)

B Extension exercises

1 Complete the dialogue with the correct verb forms.
Use the present continuous or present simple.

Joe: Hi, Sally.¹ ....*Are you listening*.... (you / listen) to music in your room?

Sally: No, I'm in the kitchen. I ² .... (cook).

Joe: Really? What ³ .... (you / cook)?

Sally: Breakfast. Mum ⁴ .... (usually / do) it but today
she ⁵ .... (chat) with her best friend online.

Joe: What about your little brother?

Sally: Well, Charlie is with Dad. They ⁶ .... (make) a model aeroplane.

Joe: Does your dad ⁷ .... (often / play) with Charlie?

Sally: Yes, he ⁸ .... (usually / do) things with us on Saturdays.
What ⁹ .... (your parents / do) this morning?

Joe: They ¹⁰ .... (walk) the dog.

2 Look at Exercise 1 and answer the questions.

1 What is Sally doing this morning?
She's cooking breakfast.

2 Who usually cooks breakfast?
....

3 Who is Sally's mum chatting with online?
....

4 What are Charlie and his dad doing?
....

5 What are Joe's parents doing this morning?
....

3 Complete the table about you. Then write sentences.

On Saturday mornings ...

	Alice	Ken	Laura and Tim	You
usually	cook breakfast	play football	walk the dog	
today	read a comic in bed	play tennis	skateboard	

Alice *usually cooks breakfast but today she* ....

Ken ....

Laura and Tim ....

I ....

C Foundation exercises

Vocabulary: Time phrases

1 Match the pictures with what Dora says. Then choose the correct words.

1 d	2	3

4	5	6

a I play football *on* / *at* Mondays.

b I always watch 'Match of the Day' *at* / *on* Sunday afternoons.

c I go skateboarding *at* / *every* the weekend.

d I go to school *every* / *in the* weekday.

e I read my book in bed *at* / *on* night.

f I sometimes go to the cinema *in the* / *every* evening.

Grammar: like/love/hate/don't like + -ing

2 Complete the sentences with *on*, *at*, *in* or *every*.

1 We watch TV ......*in*...... the evening.

2 Dora doesn't play football .... Sundays.

3 She usually chats with her friends online ....
the weekend.

4 I do homework .... day.

5 .... Sunday mornings they go to the park.

3 Complete the sentences.

1 I like ....*swimming*.... (swim).

2 She loves .... (shop)!

3 He hates .... (cook).

4 They don't like .... (dance).

5 He doesn't like .... (play) football.

6 Do you like .... (skateboard)?

7 I like .... (read) comics.

About you

4 Answer the questions about you.

1 Do you like swimming? ....*Yes, I do./No, I don't.*....

2 Do you like shopping? ....

3 Do you like getting up early? ....

4 Do you like cooking? ....

5 Does your friend like playing sports?

....

6 Does your friend like listening to music?

....

C Activation exercises

Memory check: Family members

1 Look at Claire's family tree and complete the text.

Hi!

I'm Claire. This is my cat, Holly, and here's my family tree!

Henry = Rose

Robert = Ellen   Stuart = Diana

Ricky   Olivia   Zac   Claire

Zac is my [1] _brother_. My [2] ....'s name is Diana and my
[3] ....'s name is Stuart. I've got an [4] .... and an
[5] .... Their names are Robert and Ellen. My mum is
Robert's [6] .... My [7] ....' names are Ricky and Olivia.
Henry is my [8] .... and Rose is my [9] .... My mum is
their [10] .... and Uncle Robert is their [11] ....

Vocabulary: Time phrases

2 Complete the texts.

afternoons	at	~~every~~	every	Fridays
in	in	in	on	weekends

Sophie Hi, I'm Sophie! I get up at seven
[1] _every_ day ☺. I go to school at
eight [2] .... the morning and I
come home at five [3] .... the
afternoon. I'm really into swimming,
tennis and dance. [4] .... Mondays
I go swimming and on Thursdays
[5] .... my best friend and I play
tennis. On [6] .... we go to dance
classes. That's my favourite day!

Miranda Hey, Sophie! Swimming and tennis
are my favourite sports, too! Check
out the photo of me at my school
sports day! I want to go to dance
classes but I can't. I haven't got time.

Sophie Never mind, Miranda! What other things
do you do after school?

Miranda I do my homework [7] .... the
evenings and then I watch TV or play
computer games. I go to bed at about
nine o'clock [8] .... night. At
[9] .... I go shopping with my
mum, and I visit my grandma and
granddad [10] .... Sunday.

3 Read the texts in Exercise 2 and answer
True (*T*) or *False* (*F*).

1 Sophie goes to school at seven o'clock. [F]
2 She likes tennis and swimming. ☐
3 Miranda has dance classes at school. ☐
4 She goes to bed at nine. ☐
5 She goes shopping on Saturdays. ☐

About you

4 Write to Sophie in Exercise 2.

- Introduce yourself.
- Say what your favourite sports are and when you do them.
- Say what you do at weekends.

Hi there, Sophie! ....
....
....
....
....
....
....
....
....
....
....
....
....
....

Grammar: *like/love/hate/don't like + -ing*

5 **Write sentences.**

| ☺☺ = love | ☺ = like | ☹ = don't like | ☹☹ = hate |

1 Jenny / ☺☺ / skateboard
Jenny loves skateboarding.
2 Jenny / ☹☹ / shop
....
3 Seb / ☺☺ / play football
....
4 Seb and Jenny / ☺ / dance
....

5 Luke / ☹ / dance
....
6 Luke / ☺ / watch cricket
....
7 Emma / ☹ / get up early
....
8 Emma / ☹☹ / swim
....

6 **Listen to Irek talking about life in the UK and draw faces.**

1 play football   ☺☺
2 play cricket   ....
3 wear uniform   ....
4 skateboarding   ....
5 visit museums   ....
6 watch TV   ....
7 chat to friends online   ....

7 **Look at Exercise 6 and write about Irek.**

Irek comes from Poland but he lives in London.
He loves playing football. He ....
....
....
....
....
....
....

English today

8 **Complete the dialogue.**

| Check out this photo   I'm really into music.
Luckily,   Never mind.   ~~What are you up to?~~ |

Nick: Hi, Ella. ¹ ....*What are you up to?*....
Ella: Hi, Nick. I'm going to music practice.
² ....
Nick: Do you want to come to the skate park with me after music practice?
Ella: But I can't skateboard.
Nick: ³ .... You can learn.
⁴ .... I'm a great teacher and the skate park is great, too.
⁵ .... of me skateboarding.
Ella: Thanks, Nick. See you there!

C Extension exercises

1 **Look at the table and write about the people.**

	😊😊	😊	☹️	☹️☹️
Sarah	play the trumpet	listen to jazz	listen to pop music	play sports
Jack	play cricket	play rugby	play tennis	watch football
Martha	make model trains	cook	do homework	play computer games
Lance	surf the Internet, chat with friends online	skateboard	watch TV	cook
You				

Sarah

Sarah loves playing the trumpet. She likes listening to jazz. She doesn't like listening to pop music and she hates playing sports.

Jack

....

....

....

....

....

Martha

....

....

....

....

....

Lance

....

....

....

....

....

About you

2 **Write what you like and don't like in the table in Exercise 1. Then write sentences about you.**

I love ....

....

....

....

....

....

....

....

3 **Write questions about the people in Exercise 1. Then answer the questions.**

1 **A:** *Does Lance like skateboarding?* ....

   B: Yes, he does. *He goes to the skate park every afternoon.* .... (go / skate park / every afternoon)

2 **A:** ....

   B: No, she doesn't. ....

   .... (never / listen / pop music)

3 **A:** ....

   B: Yes, he does. ....

   .... (play / cricket / Sundays)

4 **A:** ....

   B: No, she doesn't. But ....

   ....

   (do / homework / every weekday / after school)

Speaking: Talk about likes and dislikes

1 Match the sentence halves.

1 Are you OK   a him.
2 Do you want to hang   b out at my place?
3 He's   c so.
4 I can't   d amazing!
5 I don't mind   e stand him.
6 I suppose   f with that?

2 Complete the dialogue with the sentences in Exercise 1.

Carmen: Oh, hi, Diego! Hi, Maria! What are you doing?

Diego: We're playing computer games. We want to play tennis but it's raining.

Carmen: Never mind. [1] *Do you want to hang out at my place?* We can make some popcorn and watch a DVD.

Diego: Great idea! I love popcorn. Maria, [2] ....
....?

Maria: Yes, [3] ....

Diego: What kind of DVD is it?

Carmen: It's a film with Jim Carrey. What do you think? Do you like him?

Maria: Oh no! [4] .... I don't think he's funny.

Carmen: Well, we can watch an old black and white film with Charlie Chaplin.

Diego: Oh cool! I love Chaplin! [5] ....

Maria: He's OK. [6] ....

Writing: Invitations

3 Rewrite the dialogue. Use full stops, commas and capitals where necessary.

Amy: what do you want to do on saturday?
    [1] *What do you want to do on Saturday?*
....

Ben: let's go to the concert in brighton
    [2]
....

Amy: where is it? [3] ....

Ben: it's in thornton park [4] ....

Amy: what time does it start? [5] ....

Ben: it starts at eight [6] ....

Amy: let's ask jules to come with us
    [7]
....

Ben: yes i like him [8] ....

4 Look at the poster and complete the email.

Electric IcE

Thornton Park
Saturday 15th April
8.00 p.m.
Tickets: £15

One show only!

From: amyomac@123email.com
To: julesbrowne@meandmymail.com
Subject: Electric IcE concert!!!!

Hi Jules,

Do you want to come to the Electric IcE concert in Brighton? The concert is on
[1] ......*Saturday*...... 15th April at Thornton
[2] .... It starts at [3] ....
The tickets cost [4] .... Let's meet at half past seven.

I'm very excited about the concert! Electric IcE are my favourite band. I love their music – and so does Ben. He's coming to the concert, too.

I must go now. Mum is calling me for dinner!

See you!

Amy

Your turn

5 Invite your best friend to a concert to see your favourite band. Use Exercise 4 to help you.

Tell your friend:
- the name of the band and where they are playing.
- the date and time of the concert.
- how much the tickets cost.
- how you feel about the concert.

Check

1 Choose the correct answers to complete the email.

From: robzman@meandmymail.com
To: hamduggan@123email.com
Subject: News from Oz

Hi Hamish,

Thanks for your email. Do I ¹ .... living in Australia? Yes, I love it here. Check ² .... the photo of Sydney Harbour!

My new school is cool and I hang ³ .... with three friends. Rosa is Brazilian and she ⁴ .... from Rio. Eric and Janice ⁵ .... Irish. They come from Dublin. Eric's father and Janice's mother are brother and sister.

The weather in Sydney is amazing! It's sunny and hot, and I ⁶ .... at home a lot. ⁷ .... Monday afternoons I play football, and on Wednesdays Eric and I play cricket. We love it but the girls ⁸ .... like sports. Rosa's ⁹ .... dancing and she wants me to do dance classes with her! Janice loves swimming. I like it, too but Eric can't swim!!!

What ¹⁰ .... at weekends? Well, I sometimes go skateboarding. There's a great skate park near my house.

What are you up ¹¹ ....? Say hi from me to my old friends in England!

Robby

1	ⓐ like	**b** likes	**c** liking
2	**a** up	**b** in	**c** out
3	**a** up	**b** in	**c** out
4	**a** come	**b** comes	**c** is coming
5	**a** am	**b** is	**c** are
6	**a** don't stay	**b** not staying	**c** do stay
7	**a** Every	**b** At	**c** On
8	**a** isn't	**b** don't	**c** not
9	**a** into	**b** on	**c** in
10	**a** am I doing	**b** do I	**c** do I do
11	**a** on	**b** to	**c** for

Score: .... /10

2 Read the email in Exercise 1 again and answer *True* (*T*), *False* (*F*) or *Don't know* (*DK*).

1 Robby likes living in Australia. ☐ *T*
2 His new house is big. ☐
3 Eric and Janice are cousins. ☐
4 Robby plays cricket on Mondays. ☐
5 He likes dancing. ☐
6 Eric likes swimming. ☐

Score: .... /5

My score is ....!

14

2 Having fun

A Foundation exercises

Vocabulary: High numbers; Adjectives (1)

1 Complete the numbers.

1 700   seven __*hundred*__
2 492   .... hundred and
            ninety-........................
3 2,600   two thousand, six ....
4 46,377   forty-six ...., three ....
            and seventy-seven

5 8,030   eight .... and ....
6 100,000   one .... thousand
7 395,219   three hundred and ninety-five
            ...., two hundred and
            ....
8 1,000,000 a ....

2 Choose the correct words.

1 She's *old* / *young*.

2 It's *high* / *low*.

3 They're *long* / *short*.

4 It's *fast* / *slow*.

5 It's *deep* / *shallow*.

6 They're *old* / *young*.

Grammar: *how + adjective*

3 Complete the dialogue.

| deep | high | long | old | ~~shallow~~ |

Man: How ¹ __*shallow*__ is the pool here?
Attendant: It's one metre thirty.
Man: And how ² .... is the pool over there?
Attendant: It's three and a half metres deep.
Man: How ³ .... is the pool?
Attendant: It's twenty-five metres long.
Man: How ⁴ .... is that?
Attendant: It's three metres high.
Man: And how ⁵ .... is he?
Attendant: About ten years old.
Man: Wow!

A Activation exercises

Vocabulary: High numbers; Adjectives (1)

1 Match the numbers with the words.
There is one extra number.

1 The pyramid is 4,500 years old. ...b...

2 **There are 11,694 people.** ....

3 £873 ....

4 page 1013 ....

5 €650,000!!! ....

6 6,260,000 people in Britain ....

a eight hundred and seventy-three
b four thousand, five hundred
c one thousand and thirteen
d six hundred and fifty thousand
e eleven thousand, six hundred and ninety-four
f six million, two hundred and sixty thousand

2 Match the opposites.

1 long
a old
2 fast
b short
3 shallow
c high
4 young
d slow
5 low
e deep

3 Complete the texts with adjectives from Exercise 2.

Dan is ¹ .....old..... . His hair is ² .... His chair is ³ .... His bowl is ⁴ ....

Lily is ⁵ .... Her hair is ⁶ .... Her chair is ⁷ .... Her bowl is ⁸ ....

Grammar: how + adjective

4 Write Sam's questions.

Sam: Dad, ¹ ....how long is our street?.... (our street)
Dad: It's about 100 metres long.
Sam: ² .... (those trees)
Dad: They're hundreds of years old.
Sam: ³ .... (the clouds)
Dad: I think they're thousands of metres high.
Sam: ⁴ .... (our car)
Dad: It goes at 120 kilometres per hour.
Sam: ⁵ .... (the swimming pool)
Dad: I don't know how deep it is.
Sam: ⁶ .... (Grandma)
Dad: She's sixty-three.
Sam: And ⁷ .... (I)
Dad: Come on, Sam! You know!
Sam: I'm five!
Dad: No, you aren't. You're four.

5 **3 33** Listen and choose the correct answers in the quiz.

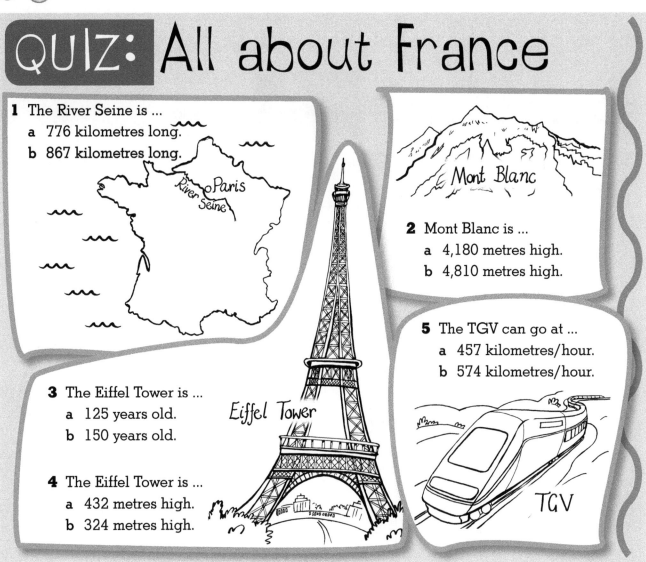

QUIZ: All about France

1 The River Seine is ...
  a 776 kilometres long.
  b 867 kilometres long.

River Seine o *Paris*

2 Mont Blanc is ...
  a 4,180 metres high.
  b 4,810 metres high.

Mont Blanc

5 The TGV can go at ...
  a 457 kilometres/hour.
  b 574 kilometres/hour.

3 The Eiffel Tower is ...
  a 125 years old.
  b 150 years old.

Eiffel Tower

4 The Eiffel Tower is ...
  a 432 metres high.
  b 324 metres high.

TGV

6 Write questions and answers about the quiz in Exercise 5.

1 A: How long is .... *the River Seine* ....?
  B: *It's seven hundred and seventy-six kilometres long.*
2 A: How high is ....?
  B: ....
  ....
3 A: How old is ....?
  B: ....
  ....
4 A: How high is ....?
  B: ....
  ....
5 A: How fast can ....?
  B: ....
  ....

English today

7 Complete the dialogue.

| I'm starving!   ~~It's awesome!~~   Let's see ... |
| on your own   Wait for me! |

Seb: What's your favourite ride here at Alton Towers?
Sophie: Oh, that's easy: Nemesis. [1] ...*It's awesome!*...
Luke: How high is it?
Sophie: [2] .... It's thirteen metres high.
Luke: I don't want to go on the ride now. I want to eat something.
Sophie: Me too. [3] ....
Seb: But I want to go on the ride.
Luke: Well, you can go [4] ....
Seb: No, I can't. Hey! [5] .... I'm coming with you!

A Extension exercises

1 Read the texts and complete the table.

Awesome rides and amazing facts!

My favourite ride is Nemesis at Alton Towers in England. It's seven hundred and sixteen metres long and thirteen metres high. It goes at eighty kilometres per hour. It can take one thousand, four hundred people per hour. I love going on this ride!

My favourite ride is Leviathan in Ontario, Canada. It's awesome! It goes at one hundred and forty-eight kilometres per hour! It's one thousand, six hundred and seventy-two metres long and ninety-three metres high.

My favourite ride is Griffon at Busch Gardens in the USA. It's nine hundred and forty-seven metres long and sixty-two metres high. It goes at one hundred and fourteen kilometres per hour. It can take one thousand, four hundred people per hour.

My favourite ride is Medusa in the USA. It can take one thousand, three hundred and fifty people per hour. It's one thousand, two hundred and fifteen metres long and forty-three metres high. It goes at ninety-eight kilometres per hour. It's amazing!

	Nemesis	Griffon	Leviathan	Medusa
How long is it?	1 _716 metres_	4	7	10 ....
How high is it?	2	5	8	43 metres
How fast is it?	3	114 kilometres per hour	9	11 ....
How many people per hour?	1,400	6		12 ....

2 Look at the table and write about Oblivion. Use Exercise 1 to help you.

Name of ride	Oblivion at Alton Towers
Country	England
Length	372 metres
Height	20 metres
Speed	109 kilometres per hour
Rides per hour	1,920

My favourite ride is Oblivion at ....

It's ....

....

It goes at ....

It can take ....

B Foundation exercises

Vocabulary: Food and drink

1 Tick (✓) the food you can see in the picture.

1 bread ✓
2 chicken ☐
3 eggs ☐
4 carrots ☐
5 peppers ☐
6 pears ☐
7 orange juice ☐
8 onions ☐
9 cheese ☐
10 yoghurt ☐

2 Match the containers with the pictures.

1 a can of cola   e
2 a carton of milk ☐
3 a bottle of water ☐
4 a box of eggs   ☐
5 a bag of onions   ☐
6 a packet of sugar ☐

a
b
c
d
e
f

Grammar: Countable and uncountable nouns; *how much/how many*

3 Write the words in the correct group.

| bread   ~~carrots~~   cheese   cucumbers   milk |
| mushrooms   orange juice   pasta   pears |
| strawberries   tomatoes   yoghurt |

Countable nouns   **Uncountable nouns**

carrots

4 Choose the correct words.

Amy: ¹(How much)/ How many milk is there?

Mark: There's a litre of milk.

Amy: ² How much / How many eggs are there?

Mark: There are six eggs.

Amy: ³ How much / How many cheese is there?

Mark: There's about fifty grams of cheese.

Amy: ⁴ How much / How many carrots are there?

Mark: There are three carrots.

Amy: ⁵ How much / How many sugar is there?

Mark: There's a packet of sugar.

Amy: ⁶ How much / How many bread is there?

Mark: Sorry, there isn't any. I was very hungry!

B Activation exercises

Vocabulary: Food and drink

1 Write the letters in the correct order to complete the puzzle. Then find the mystery word and complete the sentence.

1 lmki
2 yourgth
3 stapa
4 shif
5 ratwerssrieb
6 mottoase
7 noonis
8 crumbscue
9 gesg

Sophie loves eating ....

```
1 m i l k
2
3
4
5
6
7
8
9
```

2 Complete the words for containers and quantities.

Hi Seb,

Please go to the supermarket. We need:

* a ¹box .... of six eggs
* five ²b .... of water
* six ³c .... of cola
* two ⁴c .... of milk
* a big ⁵p .... of pasta
* one ⁶l .... of orange juice
* one ⁷k .... of tomatoes
* 500 ⁸g .... of cheese
* some yoghurt

There are some shopping ⁹b .... in the kitchen. Take them with you.

Thanks!
Mum
x

Grammar: Countable and uncountable nouns; how much/how many

3 What's in Seb's shopping bags? Choose the correct words.

1 There's a / (some) water.
2 *There's / There are* some cola.
3 *There's / There are* some pasta.
4 There's a / *some* carton of orange juice.
5 *There's / There are* eight tomatoes.
6 There's a / *some* cheese.
7 There's a / *some* pot of yoghurt.

4 Look at Exercises 2 and 3 and complete the sentences. What did Seb forget to buy?

Seb, there aren't any ¹ ....
And there isn't any ² ....

Oh! Sorry, Mum.

5 Complete the dialogue with *a*, *an* or *some*.

Mum: We need ¹ ....*a*.... carton of orange juice, ² .... litre of milk and ³ .... yoghurt.

Emma: What about dinner tonight? We can't have orange juice, milk and yoghurt for dinner!

Mum: Let's get ⁴ .... chicken and ⁵ .... mushrooms. Oh, and ⁶ .... onion.

Emma: Oh! Look at those pears! Can I have ⁷ .... pear, Mum?

Mum: Yes, put ⁸ .... pears in this bag. And Dad loves strawberries. We can have ⁹ .... strawberries after dinner.

6 Write questions and answers with *how much* and *how many*.

We need some things from the supermarket.

1 (pears? four)
   A: *How many pears do we need?*
   B: *We need four pears.*

2 (Greek yoghurt? 500 g)
   A: ....
   B: ....

3 (water? two bottles)
   A: ....
   B: ....

4 (red peppers? ten)
   A: ....
   B: ....

5 (milk? 3 l)
   A: ....
   B: ....

6 (cheese? 300 g)
   A: ....
   B: ....

7 (tomatoes? 2 kg)
   A: ....
   B: ....

8 (pasta? one packet)
   A: ....
   B: ....

9 (eggs? six)
   A: ....
   B: ....

10 (orange juice? two cartons)
   A: ....
   B: ....

7 Match Liam's questions with Carrie's answers.

Liam and Carrie are chatting online.

¹ .*d*.

Hey, Liam! My favourite pizza is cheese and tomato. And it's very easy to make.

² ....

First, you need a pizza base.

³ ....

Next, you need some tomatoes. How many tomatoes have you got?

⁴ ....

OK, five is just right.

⁵ ....

You don't need peppers for this recipe but you need some cheese.

⁶ ....

About 100 grams. Grate it on top of the pizza. Off you go! Enjoy! ☺

a How much cheese?

b Mmm, yummy! What do I need?

c I've got five.

d Hi, Carrie. I want to make a pizza but Mum's not at home and I never cook. What's a good pizza?

e What about red peppers? Are they good on pizza?

f OK. I've got one here. What next?

B Extension exercises

1 Complete the recipes. Write one word in each gap.

Salad

Ingredients
- ✔ [1] *some* carrots
- ✔ [2] .... big cucumber
- ✔ [3] .... small red peppers
- ✔ a small [4] .... of Greek yoghurt

Instructions
Cut up the carrots, the cucumber and the three peppers. Put them in a bowl. Then add the Greek yoghurt and mix.

Pasta with chicken and mushrooms

Ingredients
- ✔ 250 [5] .... of chicken
- ✔ [6] .... onion
- ✔ some mushrooms
- ✔ a large [7] .... of pasta

Instructions
Cook the chicken and cut it into pieces. Cut the onion and the mushrooms and cook them. Put the pasta in hot water and cook it. Mix the chicken, mushrooms and pasta.

Fruit salad

Ingredients
- ✔ about 400 [8] .... of strawberries
- ✔ two large [9] ....
- ✔ some orange [10] ....
- ✔ vanilla ice cream

Instructions
Cut the strawberries and pears. Mix them and add orange juice. Put the mixture in the fridge for an hour. Serve with vanilla ice cream. Yummy!

2 Match the pictures with the recipes in Exercise 1. There is one extra picture.

1 _Pasta with chicken and mushrooms_

2 ....

3 ....

4 ....

About you

3 What is your favourite food? How do you make it?

My favourite food is ....

You make it with ....

You need ....

....

....

....

Speaking: Order food and drink

1 Write the words in the correct order.

1 [some] [like] [you] [ice cream?] [would]

Would you like some ice cream? ....

2 [have] [I] [please?] [some water,] [can]

....

3 [like] [would] [drink?] [what] [you] [to]

....

4 [scoops] [how] [many] [you] [like?] [would]

....

5 [you] [are] [order?] [ready] [to]

....

6 [you] [excuse] [any] [me.] [have]
[tomato ketchup?] [got]

....

2 Match the questions 1–6 in Exercise 1 with the answers a–f.

a Of course. There's a bottle over there. ....6....
b Can I have two, please? ....
c Can I have a glass of milk, please? ....
d Yes, I'd like some chocolate ice cream, please. ....
e Yes, I'd like the pasta with mushrooms, please. ....
f Yes, sure. Here you are. ....

Your turn

3 Complete the dialogue. Use the words in brackets or your own ideas.

Waiter: Are you ready to order?
Seb: ¹ (chicken and chips) ....
Luke: ² (the same) ....
Waiter: ³ (drink) ....
Seb: ⁴ (two glasses of water) ....
Waiter: Here you are.
Luke: Thanks.
Waiter: ⁵ (dessert) ....
Seb: ⁶ (vanilla ice cream) ....
Waiter: ⁷ (scoops) ....
Seb: Two, please.
Luke: ⁸ (the same) ....

Writing: A recipe

4 Complete the recipe with *first*, *then* and *finally* and add commas where necessary.

Recipe of the day

Ingredients
- 100 g mushrooms
- 3 red peppers
- 1 small onion
- 50 g cheese
- bread

Instructions
¹ .... cut the mushrooms the red peppers and the onion and cook them in a frying pan. ² .... put the mixture on the bread. ³ .... grate the cheese over the mixture. Put the bread on a plate with a green salad. Yummy!

Your turn

5 Write the ingredients and instructions for a recipe. Use the pictures and Exercise 4 to help you.

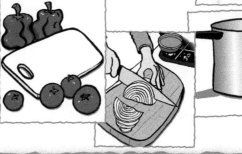

Recipe of the day: pasta with tomatoes, red peppers and onion

Ingredients
- 1 ....*packet of pasta*....
- 2 ....
- 4 big ....
- 1 ....
- some ....

Instructions
First, ...
....
....
....
....

Check

1 Complete the dialogue. Write one word in each gap.

Mum: OK, Seb. Let's buy ¹ ......_some_...... food for the weekend.

Seb: What do we need, Mum?

Mum: Let's see ... We need ² .... pasta.

Seb: How ³ .... pasta do we need?

Mum: A ⁴ .... Oh, and we need about 400 ⁵ .... of cheese and ⁶ .... mushrooms.

Seb: Here, Mum.

Mum: Now, we haven't got ⁷ .... vegetables at home. Let's get ⁸ .... cucumber and ⁹ .... red peppers.

Seb: How ¹⁰ .... red peppers?

Mum: Mm ... three.

Seb: Mum, can we get a ¹¹ .... of orange juice, too?

Mum: Of course, Seb. And I want a ¹² .... of cola. I'm thirsty.

I kg of pasta

cheese

mushrooms

a cucumber

red peppers

Score: .... /11

2 Choose the correct answers.

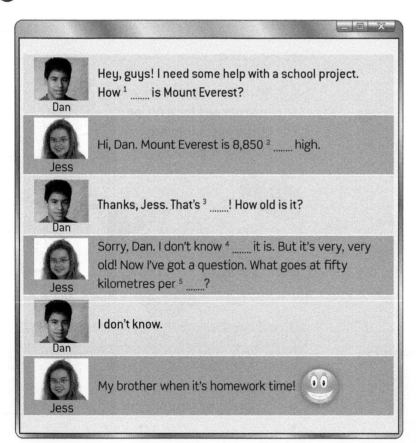

Dan: Hey, guys! I need some help with a school project. How ¹ ...... is Mount Everest?

Jess: Hi, Dan. Mount Everest is 8,850 ² ...... high.

Dan: Thanks, Jess. That's ³ ......! How old is it?

Jess: Sorry, Dan. I don't know ⁴ ...... it is. But it's very, very old! Now I've got a question. What goes at fifty kilometres per ⁵ ......?

Dan: I don't know.

Jess: My brother when it's homework time!

1 a metres	**(b)** high	**c** low
2 a kilograms	**b** grams	**c** metres
3 a awesome	**b** no way	**c** wow
4 a how deep	**b** how high	**c** how old
5 a week	**b** hour	**c** year

Score: .... /4

My score is ....!

3 Past times

A Foundation exercises

Vocabulary: Professions

1 Write the professions.

actress	author	comedian	composer	~~dancer~~	film director
inventor	magician	painter	scientist	singer	

1 .... *dancer* ....

2 ....

3 ....

4 ....

5 ....

6 ....

7 ....

8 ....

9 ....

10 ....

11 ....

Grammar: Past simple: *be*

2 Complete the tables.

+	
I ¹ ....*was*.......	very funny.
You ²	sad.
She ³	a great singer.
We were	happy.
They ⁴	brilliant scientists.

?	
Were you here yesterday?	Yes, I was./No, I ⁵ ....
⁶ .... they inventors?	Yes, they ⁷ ..../ No, they weren't.

3 Choose the correct words.

1 Walt Disney *was* / were a director.
2 Houdini *wasn't* / weren't an actor.
3 *Was* / *Were* you at school at ten o'clock?
4 I *was* / *were* born in 2001.
5 *Was* / *Were* the Wright brothers inventors?
6 Marilyn Monroe *wasn't* / *weren't* a film director.

A Activation exercises

Vocabulary: Professions; Dates

1 Complete the crossword.

Across

1 Harry Houdini was a .... His magic tricks were fantastic.
5 Adele is a great .... Her songs are brilliant.
9 Mozart was a .... I love his music.
10 Vincent van Gogh was a .... His pictures of flowers are amazing.
11 Marilyn Monroe was a great .... She was very famous.

Down

2 The Wright brothers were the .... of the aeroplane.
3 Walt Disney was a famous American film ....
4 Shakespeare was a very famous English ....
6 Laurel and Hardy were famous .... They were very funny.
7 Albert Einstein was a great .... He was born in Germany.
8 Michael Jackson was an amazing .... His songs are great, too.

	¹m	a	g	²i	c	i	a	n

(crossword grid with numbered cells 1–11)

2 Write the years in words.

1 .... *two thousand and four* ....
2 ....
3 ....
4 ....
5 ....
6 ....
7 ....
8 ....

Grammar: Past simple: *be*

3 Choose the correct words.

My mother's parents ¹was /**were** from England and my mother ²was / were born here in 1971. My dad's parents ³wasn't / weren't born in England. They ⁴was / were born in South Africa, and my dad ⁵was / were born there in 1970. My sister and I ⁶was / were born there, too – in Durban. Durban is a fantastic city and we ⁷was / were happy there. But England is cool, too.

4 Match the questions with the answers.

1 Was Luke's dad born in South Africa?   ..c..
2 Were his father's parents from England?   ....
3 Was his mother's mother from South Africa?   ....
4 Was his mother born in 1971?   ....
5 Was his father born in 1971?   ....
6 Were Luke and his sister born in South Africa?   ....

a Yes, she was.   c Yes, he was.   e Yes, they were.
b No, he wasn't.   d No, she wasn't.   f No, they weren't.

5 Write sentences with *was*, *wasn't*, *were* or *weren't*.

1 Laurence Olivier: actor ✓ magician ✗   *Laurence Olivier was an actor. He wasn't a magician.*
2 Maria Callas and Tito Gobbi: singers ✓ composers ✗   ....
3 Charles Dickens: author ✓ painter ✗   ....
4 Beethoven and Bach: composers ✓ painters ✗   ....
5 Marie Curie: scientist ✓ dancer ✗   ....
6 Raphael: painter ✓ singer ✗   ....
7 Anna Pavlova and Vaslav Nijinsky: dancers ✓ scientists ✗   ....
8 Thomas Edison: inventor ✓ film director ✗   ....

6 Look at the fact files and complete the dialogue with *was*, *wasn't*, *were* or *weren't*.

Name: Galileo Galilei
Job: scientist
Born: 1564, Italy
Nationality: Italian

Name: Enrico Fermi
Job: scientist
Born: 1901, Italy
Nationality: American

Emma: Who are the people in the pictures, Luke?
Luke: They [1] *were* both scientists. I'm writing about them for my History project.
Emma: What [2] .... their names?
Luke: This man's name [3] .... Galileo Galilei and that man's name [4] .... Enrico Fermi.
Emma: [5] .... they Spanish?
Luke: No, they [6] .... Galileo [7] .... Italian and Fermi [8] .... American. But Fermi [9] .... born in the United States.

Emma: Where [10] .... he born?
Luke: In Italy.
Emma: When [11] .... Galileo born?
Luke: In 1564.
Emma: And Fermi?
Luke: In 1901.
Emma: Are they famous?
Luke: Yes, he and Galileo [12] .... both brilliant scientists and they are very famous for their work.

7 Write the words in the correct order to make questions about the scientists in Luke's project.

1 the scientists' | were | what | names?   *What were the scientists' names?*
2 was | who | in the photo? | the old man   ....
3 born? | Galileo | when | was   ....
4 was | he | why | famous?   ....
5 Galileo and Fermi | were | Spanish?   ....
6 where | from | was | Enrico Fermi?   ....

A Extension exercises

1 Write about the people.

J.R.R. Tolkien

English author

Born: South Africa, 1892

Famous books: *The Hobbit, The Lord of the Rings*

J.R.R. Tolkien was a famous English author. He was born in South Africa in eighteen ninety-two. His famous books were *The Hobbit* and *The Lord of the Rings*.

Chico, Harpo and Groucho Marx

American comedians

Born: New York City, 1887 (Chico), 1888 (Harpo), 1890 (Groucho)

Famous films: *Horse Feathers, Duck Soup, A Night at the Opera, A Day at the Races*

....

....

....

....

....

....

Lucille Ball

American comedian and actress

Born: United States, 1911

Famous TV programmes: *I Love Lucy, The Lucy Show, Here's Lucy, Life With Lucy*

....

....

....

....

....

About you

2 Answer the questions about you and your family.

1 Where were your grandparents from?

....

2 Where was your mum/dad born?

....

3 When was your mum/dad born?

....

4 Where were you born?

....

5 When were you born?

....

6 Were you a pretty baby?

....

Vocabulary: TV programmes

1 Complete the words.

1 qu_i_z sh_o_w

2 d_o_c_u_m_e_nt_a_ry

3 c_a_rt___n

4 dr_a_m_a   s_e_r_ie__s

5 th_e_   n_e_ws

6 r_ea__l_ty   sh_o_w

7 s___p   _p_r_

8 c_o_m_e_dy

9 t_a_l_nt   sh_o_w

Grammar: Past simple: regular verbs

2 Choose the correct words.

1 I *watch* / (*watched*) my favourite TV programme last night.
2 Luke *didn't missed* / *didn't miss* the quiz show yesterday. He loves that show.
3 '*Did you like* / *Did you liked* the cartoon?' 'Yes, I *did* / *didn't*.'
4 What *did you watch* / *did you watched* last night?
5 Sophie *answer* / *answered* all the questions.
6 Seb *didn't* / *not* open the window.
7 *Your friends like* / *Did your friends like* the film?
8 My friend's team *didn't cook* / *not cook* fish. They *cook* / *cooked* pasta.
9 How many questions *asked they* / *did they ask*?
10 The documentary was amazing! We *love* / *loved* it.

About you

3 Answer the questions about you.

1 Did you watch TV last night?
   Yes, I did./No, I didn't.
2 Did you watch your favourite programme?
   ....
3 Did your parents watch the news last night?
   ....
4 Did you talk to your best friend on the phone yesterday?
   ....
5 Did you cook dinner last night?
   ....
6 Did you stay at home yesterday evening?
   ....
7 Did you help your mum in the kitchen yesterday?
   ....

B Activation exercises

Vocabulary: TV programmes

1 **What programmes are the people talking about? Write the words.**

| cartoon | comedy | documentary | drama series | quiz show | ~~reality show~~ | soap opera | the news |

> The people in the programme aren't actors. They want to be famous singers.

1 ...._reality show_........

> It's very funny! I love the cat and mouse!

2 ....

> That's my favourite actor. He's really funny! And the story is funny, too.

3 ....

> Janet loves Bob but Bob loves Janet's sister, Megan. Megan loves Rick but Rick loves Janet ...

4 ....

> Mum and Dad listen to it every evening. They want to know what's happening in the world.

5 ....

> The actors are good but the story is sad.

6 ....

> This programme is interesting. The fish in the sea are beautiful!

7 ....

> It's my favourite programme. People answer questions and sometimes they win a lot of money.

8 ....

Grammar: Past simple: regular verbs

2 **Match the sentence halves.**

1 Luke and Emma watched
2 What did their dad
3 Their mum cooked
4 Did Luke miss
5 Did the woman on the quiz show
6 Emma helped
7 Their mum didn't
8 Did you talk

a a fantastic dinner last night.
b answer all the questions?
c cook for dinner last weekend?
d his favourite programme on TV yesterday?
e her friend with her homework.
f their favourite programme on TV last night.
g to your friend yesterday?
h watch the news on TV last night.

3 **Complete Sophie's blog with the correct verb forms. Use the past simple.**

My weekend

Last Friday I was very, very tired and I ¹ ......_stayed_...... (stay) at home. I ² .... (not visit) my friends and I ³ .... (not help) my dad in the garden. I ⁴ .... (not talk) to Seb on the phone but I ⁵ .... (play) with my cat, Buster. I ⁶ .... (helped) Mum with the dinner and then I ⁷ .... (watch) TV. At nine o'clock I ⁸ .... (watch) a reality show but I ⁹ .... (not like) it. I ¹⁰ .... (hate) it!

4 **Look at the table and write questions and answers about Dave, Jade and Cathy.**

Last Friday ...

	Dave	Jade	Cathy
visit cousins	✗	✓	✓
talk to friends	✗	✗	✓
cook dinner	✓	✓	✗
watch the news	✓	✗	✗

1 Dave / visit / his cousins?
A: *Did Dave visit his cousins?*
B: *No, he didn't.*
2 Cathy / visit / her cousins?
A: ....
B: ....
3 Dave and Jade / talk / to their friends?
A: ....
B: ....

4 Cathy / cook / dinner?
A: ....
B: ....
5 Dave / watch / the news?
A: ....
B: ....
6 Jade / watch / the news?
A: ....
B: ....

5 **Complete the dialogue with the correct verb forms. Use the past simple.**

Liz: Hi, Tom! Where were you last night? I wanted to ask you a question about homework but you ¹ *didn't answer* (not answer) your phone.

Tom: I was at my granny's house. I wanted to watch the new drama series but I ² .... (miss) it. I ³ .... (help) my granny with the dinner. ⁴ .... (you / watch) it?

Liz: Yes, I ⁵ .... But I ⁶ .... (not like) it. What ⁷ .... (you / watch)?

Tom: I ⁸ .... (not watch) TV.

Liz: Oh. And what ⁹ .... (you and your granny / cook)?

Tom: Fish and vegetables. It was yummy!

English today

6 **Put the dialogue in the correct order.**

Yes, I answered all of them. They were so easy! ....
Well, I also wanted to watch a film on another channel. It was fantastic! ...8...
Did you watch TV last night? ....
Yes, I watched *The Good and the Beautiful*. ....
Hi, Sophie. Did you answer the questions for Maths homework? ...1...
Well, Cliff wanted to go to Paris with Susan but Susan didn't want to go with him because she loves Thorpe, and then ... I don't know. ....
Come on, Sophie! Why? ....
I missed it. What happened? ....

B Extension exercises

1 Complete the dialogues with the correct verb forms. Use the past simple.

	Channel 1	Channel 2
6 p.m.	**Walking with Kings** Val Evans walks with lions in the Kruger Park, South Africa.	**Funky Scientists** Tonight six clever people invent cars. And the winner is ...?
7 p.m.	**It's in the Box!** Fun with Kenny Adams and £50,000 for the winner!	**The Long Road Home** Roland wants to see Dolores but does Dolores want to see Roland?
8 p.m.	**News at Eight** with Bob Morton	**People in the News** Tonight Hollywood actress Zoe Little talks with Meg Rose.

Luke: ¹ ....*What did you watch*....... (what / you / watch) last night?

Seb: ² .... (I / watch) *Walking with Kings*.

Luke: What was it about?

Seb: It was about lions in Africa.

Luke: Oh no! ³ .... (I / miss) it!
⁴ .... (you / like) it?

Seb: Yes, ⁵ .... It was fantastic!

Kim: ⁶ .... (you / watch) *It's in the Box!* last night?

Emma: No, ⁷ .... (I / talk) to Elena for an hour.

Kim: An hour! ⁸ .... (what / you / talk) about?

Emma: Homework. Well, what happened?

Kim: ⁹ .... (a man / open) the first box.
¹⁰ .... (Carol James / ask) him an easy question but ¹¹ .... (he / not answer) it.

2 Read the dialogues in Exercise 1 again and choose the correct answers.

1 What did Seb watch last night?
  a a cartoon   **b** a documentary   **c** a drama series

2 What did Emma do last night?
  a She did her homework.   **b** She watched a quiz.   **c** She talked to a friend.

3 What did Kim watch?
  a a quiz show   **b** a talk show   **c** a soap opera

About you

3 Answer the questions about you.

1 What programmes did you watch on TV last night? ....

2 Did you like them? ....

3 Did your parents watch TV last night? ....

4 What did they watch? ....

C Foundation exercises

Vocabulary: Time expressions

1 Choose the correct words.

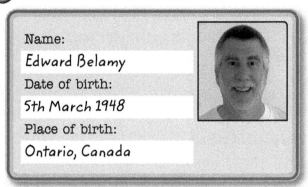

Name:
Edward Belamy
Date of birth:
5th March 1948
Place of birth:
Ontario, Canada

1 My grandfather was born in *1940 /(the 1940s)*.

Thursday
Watch quiz show.

Friday

2 Today is Friday. I watched the quiz show *yesterday / ago*.

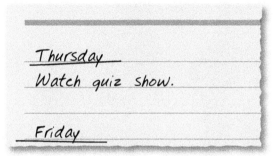

| 1 Sun | 2 Mon | 3 Tues | 4 Wed | 5 Thurs | 6 Fri | 7 Sat |
| HOLIDAY ☺ |
| 8 Sun | 9 Mon | 10 Tues | 11 Wed | 12 Thurs | 13 Fri | 14 Sat |
| SCHOOL ☹ |

3 School started this week. I was on holiday *last / yesterday* week.

| 24 Sun | 25 Mon | 26 Tues Mum's birthday! | 27 Wed |
| 28 Thurs | 29 Fri | 30 Sat Mum's birthday party today! | |

4 Mum's birthday party is today but her birthday was four days *ago / last*, on 26th May.

Grammar: Past simple: irregular verbs

2 Write the verbs in the correct columns.

ate	became	bought	come	did	drank
go	got up	~~had~~	made	meet	ride	saw
took	was	wear			

Present	Past simple	Present	Past simple
have	1 *had*	be	9 ....
see	2	10	wore
3	rode	get up	11 ....
buy	4	12	met
5	came	do	13 ....
make	6	become	14 ....
drink	7	15	went
eat	8	take	16 ....

3 Complete the tables.

+
I wore jeans.
He 1 *wore* jeans.
–
I didn't 2 .... jeans.
He 3 .... wear jeans.

?	
4 .... you wear jeans?	Yes, I did./ No, I 5 ....
Did he 6 .... jeans?	Yes, he 7 ..../ No, he 8 ....
What 9 .... they ....?	They 10 .... jeans.

C Activation exercises

Vocabulary: Time expressions

1 Choose the correct words. Then tick (✓) the sentences that are true for you.

1 I played football two days *yesterday / ago*. ☐

2 I was in town *yesterday / ago*. ☐

3 I saw a great film *weekend last / last weekend*. ☐

4 My mother was born *on / in* the 1980s. ☐

5 I had a great holiday *last year / year last*. ☐

6 I went to school *last / yesterday*. ☐

Grammar: Past simple: irregular verbs

2 Complete the text with the correct verb forms. Use the present simple.

become	come	do	~~get up~~	go	have	see	wear

I ¹ ....*get up*..... at seven o'clock on weekdays. I ² .... jeans and a T-shirt. I ³ .... orange juice and toast for breakfast. I ⁴ .... to school at eight. I like school because I ⁵ .... my friends there. Sometimes my friends ⁶ .... to my house after school and we ⁷ .... our homework together. I want to ⁸ .... a doctor and I study a lot.

3 Match the sentence halves.

1 Luke's dad comes home late on weekdays

2 Emma does her homework every day

3 Emma likes wearing jeans

4 Seb rides his bike to school

5 Kim often makes new friends at parties

6 Luke and Emma eat fruit for breakfast

7 Seb gets up early on weekdays

a but last Monday he got up very late.

b and he rode his bike yesterday.

c and she did her homework yesterday.

d but last Friday he came home early.

e and she made a friend last night.

f and they ate bananas yesterday.

g but yesterday she wore a dress.

4 Choose the correct answers.

It's a fact!

1 People .... the first colour photos about 160 years ago.
   a take   **ⓑ** took

2 The composer Johann Sebastian Bach .... twenty-one children.
   a had   **b** have

3 William Pitt the Younger was twenty-four years old when he .... Prime Minister of Britain in 1783.
   a became   **b** become

4 The Maya people of Mexico .... chocolate 2,000 years ago.
   a drink   **b** drank

5 People .... the first computers for their homes in the 1970s.
   a buy   **b** bought

6 People .... glasses for the first time about 750 years ago.
   a wear   **b** wore

5 (3/34) **Listen to Mark and Sally Harris talking to their teacher about their holiday and tick (✓) the things they did.**

1 go to:	South Africa	☐	Spain	☐
2 wear:	jeans, shirts and jackets	☐	shorts and T-shirts	☐
3 buy:	new swimming costumes	☐	walking shoes	☐
4 see:	elephants	☐	leopards	☐
5 take photos of:	animals	☐	Table Mountain	☐
6 go:	swimming	☐	shopping	☐

6 **Write about Mark and Sally. Use Exercise 5 to help you.**

Last August, Mark and Sally Harris went to South Africa.
They didn't go to Spain. They ....
....
....
....
....
....
....

7 **Write questions and answers about Mark and Sally. Use Exercise 5 to help you.**

1 Mark and Sally / go / Spain / last August?
A: *Did Mark and Sally go to Spain last August?*
B: *No, they didn't.*

2 where / they / go?
A: ....
B: ....

3 they / wear / shorts and T-shirts?
A: ....
B: ....

4 what / they / wear?
A: ....
B: ....

5 their mother / buy / them swimming costumes?
A: ....
B: ....

6 what animals / they / see?
A: ....
B: ....

7 they / go / shopping?
A: ....
B: ....

C Extension exercises

1 Complete the sentences with the correct verb forms. Use the past simple.

Life in the past!

- British people [1] _didn't eat_ (not eat) pizzas sixty years ago. Pizzas only [2] .... (become) popular in the UK in the 1970s.
- People on the island of Santorini in Greece [3] .... (have) hot and cold water in their houses 3,600 years ago.
- In the 1700s English girls [4] .... (not go) to school. Only boys [5] .... (go) to school.
- People in Europe [6] .... (not eat) potatoes and they [7] .... (not drink) orange juice 1,000 years ago. Potatoes [8] .... (come) to Europe from South America and oranges [9] .... (come) from Asia.
---

2 Read the texts and complete the table.

Cora

I came to the party at six. I wore a white T-shirt, black jeans and black shoes. I ate two burgers and birthday cake but I didn't drink orange juice. I went home at nine.

Dora

I didn't come to the party at half past six. I didn't wear blue jeans. I wore a white T-shirt and black shoes. I drank two glasses of orange juice and I ate birthday cake and chips. I went home with Cora.

Kate

I rode to the party on my bike and I came early. I wore black trousers and a shirt but the shirt wasn't black. It was pink. I ate cake and chips, and I drank apple juice. I went home at nine.

Nora

Dora and Kate came to the party before me. I wore trousers and a white shirt. I drank apple juice and I ate birthday cake. I went home late. I was the last person at the party!

Name	Clothes	Food	Time
[1] ....Cora.........	T-shirt, jeans	burgers, cake	6.00–9.00 p.m.
[2]	shirt and trousers	cake, chips and apple juice	5.45–9.00 p.m.
[3]	shirt and trousers	cake, apple juice	6.30–9.15 p.m.
[4]	T-shirt and trousers	cake, chips, orange juice	5.45–9.00 p.m.

3 Answer the questions about the girls in Exercise 2.

1 Where did Cora, Dora, Nora and Kate go last night?
   They went to a party.
2 What did Cora wear to the party?
   ....
3 What did Kate eat?
   ....
4 What did Nora drink?
   ....
5 Who did Dora go home with?
   ....
6 What time did Kate go home?
   ....

About you

4 Answer the questions about you.

1 What time did you get up this morning?
   ....
2 What did you have for breakfast?
   ....
3 What did you wear?
   ....
4 Did you go to school?
   ....
5 What did you do last Saturday?
   ....
6 Did you have a good time last Saturday?
   ....

Speaking: Talk about your weekend

1 Put the words in the correct order. Then ask and answer with your partner.

1 your was weekend? how
How was your weekend?
....

2 your holiday like? was what
....

3 did the do at what weekend? you
....

4 enjoy did party? you the
....

2 Choose the correct answers to complete the dialogue.

Luke: Hi, Seb. How was your weekend?
Seb: ¹ ....
Luke: What did you do?
Seb: ² .... We had a fantastic time. What about your weekend?
Luke: ³ .... I wanted to go to the cinema but we stayed at home. On Saturday night my mum made popcorn and we watched a black and white film on TV.
Seb: What about you, Kim?
Kim: I went to the cinema with my cousin. We saw *The Inventors*.
Luke: What was it like?
Kim: ⁴ .... I want to see it again.
Seb: Let's all go on Friday.
Luke: Cool!

1 a I stayed at home.
    b It was great!
    c I missed it.
2 a My dad and I went camping.
    b My dad and I want to go camping.
    c My dad and I like camping.
3 a I went home.
    b It was brilliant!
    c It was a bit boring.
4 a Yes, it was.
    b I didn't enjoy it.
    c It was great!

Writing: Describe a TV programme

3 Complete the sentences with *or*, *and* or *but*.

1 Danny wants to become a film director ..*and*.. make films in Hollywood.
2 I like quiz shows .... I don't like reality shows.
3 He didn't like the talent show .... the comedy.
4 I went to Anna's party .... I didn't enjoy it.
5 Linda watched the news at nine .... then the drama series at ten.
6 I wanted to watch the film .... I missed it.

4 Complete Mia's blog with *and* or *but*.

> 6 p.m. *Chester*
> by Dick Dark
> Tonight's episode:
> *Where did Fred go?*

Mia   My favourite TV programme

My favourite TV programme is a cartoon, *Chester*. It is very popular with young children ¹ ..*but*.. adults ² .... old people love it, too. In my family we all watch it: Mum, Dad, my little brother Jason ³ .... my grandpa.

Chester is a cat ⁴ .... he lives with a lot of other animals on a farm. In every episode the animals get into trouble ⁵ .... Chester is clever ⁶ .... he helps them. Chester has a good friend, Lady the bulldog, ⁷ .... Lady helps Chester. In this cartoon the people and animals don't talk ⁸ .... they sometimes make noises.

My favourite episode was *Where did Fred go?* In this episode, Fred, a very old horse, ate some magic carrots ⁹ .... he became very, very small, like a mouse. It was very funny ¹⁰ .... I laughed and laughed!

Your turn

5 Write about your favourite TV cartoon. Use Exercise 4 to help you.

● Say who the main characters are and what they do.
● Say what happens in your favourite episode. Is it funny or sad? Why?

Check

1 Choose the correct answers to complete the email.

From: valdegal@123email.com
To: lulugregson@123email.com
Subject: Weekend

Hi Lulu,

Thanks for your email! I didn't ¹ ...... anywhere ² ...... Friday evening. I ³ ...... at home and watched a documentary about New York ⁴ ...... the 1930s. It was a bit ⁵ ...... but I loved the film at nine o'clock! I want to become a film ⁶ ...... one day and make films.

On Saturday morning I ⁷ ...... my dad in his shop and then I ⁸ ...... Alan and Eva in town.

⁹ ...... was your weekend? ¹⁰ ...... camping? What ¹¹ ...... it like?

Write soon.

Valerie

1	**(a)** go	**b** went	**c** not went	7 **a** help	**b** helped	**c** helping
2	**a** ago	**b** yesterday	**c** last	8 **a** meet	**b** met	**c** did meet
3	**a** stay	**b** stayed	**c** did stay	9 **a** Where	**b** What	**c** How
4	**a** on	**b** at	**c** in	10 **a** You go	**b** You went	**c** Did you go
5	**a** boring	**b** great	**c** easy	11 **a** was	**b** do	**c** did
6	**a** singer	**b** composer	**c** director			

Score: ...... /10

2 Choose the correct answers.

1 Did you enjoy your weekend?
  a I went to the cinema.
  b We met our friends in town.
  (c) Yes, I did. It was brilliant!

2 How was your weekend?
  a It was fantastic!
  b I'm fine, thanks.
  c It was so easy!

3 I went camping. What about you?
  a I loved it.
  b We enjoyed it.
  c Anna and I went shopping.

4 What happened?
  a I don't know. I didn't watch it.
  b Come on, Greg!
  c Did you see Greg?

5 Where did you meet them?
  a Three months ago.
  b At the party.
  c Yesterday.

6 Did she invent that?
  a Yes, she invented. She's an inventor.
  b Yes, she invented. She isn't an inventor.
  c Yes, she did. She's an inventor.

Score: ...... /5

My score is ....!

38

4 It's a musical world.

A Foundation exercises

Vocabulary: Types of music and musical instruments

1 Find and write eight words for musical instruments.

K	G	U	I	T	A	R	Y	W
E	A	D	I	R	O	E	S	U
Y	N	D	R	U	M	S	A	T
B	A	S	S	M	T	N	K	F
O	E	S	J	P	I	A	N	O
A	H	V	L	E	Y	L	C	R
R	T	F	O	T	P	R	M	D
D	V	I	O	L	I	N	E	D
S	A	X	O	P	H	O	N	E

1 ....*guitar*............ 5 ....
2 .... 6 ....
3 .... 7 ....
4 .... 8 ....

2 Complete the words for types of music.

1 p.o.p
2 r.....k
3 f..l...
4 r...p
5 h...p .....o....
6 cl..... .....i..... l
7 .....zz
8 b....u.........

Grammar: Past simple: regular and irregular verbs (2)

3 Write the verbs in the correct columns.

| ~~changed~~ give meet played put started |
| support want went won |

Present: regular verbs	Past simple: regular verbs
change	1 ....*changed*.............
2	supported
3	wanted
start	4 ....
play	5 ....

Present: irregular verbs	Past simple: irregular verbs
put	6 ....
go	7 ....
8	met
win	9 ....
10	gave

4 Complete the answers with verbs from Exercise 3.

1 **A:** What did Luke want to do yesterday?
  B: He .....*wanted*....... to go to the cinema.
2 **A:** Who went to Brighton yesterday?
  B: Seb .... to Brighton.
3 **A:** Who did Seb meet in Brighton?
  B: He .... some friends.
4 **A:** Where did Sophie go yesterday?
  B: She .... to Luke's house.
5 **A:** Who won a competition last week?
  B: Emma .... a competition.

A Activation exercises

Vocabulary: Types of music and musical instruments

1 Match the pictures with the sentences. There is one extra picture.

1 | c

2 |

3 |

4 |

5 |

a They love rap.
b She hates jazz.

c He's a pop singer in a boy band.
d She plays classical music.

2 Complete the crossword.

² k e y ³ b o a r d s

Across
2
4
5
7
8

Down
1
3
6

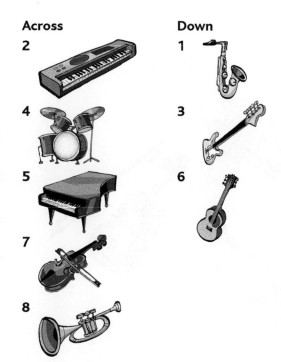

Grammar: Past simple: regular and irregular verbs (2); Wh- questions; Subject questions

3 Choose the correct words.

My blog   **by Tom Reese**

My dad's a rock star!

When my dad was fifteen, he ¹*want /*(*wanted*) to start a rock band. He ²*posted / post* an ad on the school's notice board. Some kids from his school, Amy, Jim and Hayley, ³*answer / answered* it, and my dad ⁴*met / meet* them in a café a week later. They ⁵*start / started* a band called The Banshees. They ⁶*won / win* second prize in a talent show and then they ⁷*change / changed* the band's name. I ⁸*asked / ask* my dad about this and he said Amy and Hayley didn't like The Banshees. Now they're The Staxx. My dad's the lead singer and he's famous!

4 Match the questions about Tom's dad from Exercise 3 with the answers.

1 What did Tom's dad want to start?   ..*f*..
2 What did he post?   ....
3 Who answered the ad?   ....
4 When did Tom's dad meet Amy, Jim and Hayley?   ....
5 Where did he meet them?   ....
6 What did they win?   ....
7 Why did they change the band's name?   ....

a Amy, Jim and Hayley answered the ad.
b They changed it because Amy and Hayley didn't like it.
c He met them a week later.
d He met them in a café.
e He posted an ad on the school's notice board.
f He wanted to start a rock band.
g They won second prize in a talent show.

5 Complete the newspaper article with the correct verb forms. Use the past simple.

answer	give	make	meet	post	start
support	~~want~~	want			

Molly and The One Hundred

Young musician Molly Adams ¹ ___wanted___ to start a band but not a rock band or pop group. She ² _____ to play classical music.

So Molly, who's thirteen, ³ _____ an ad on her school's notice board. 'It was amazing!' she said. 'Ninety-nine students ⁴ _____ the ad! I ⁵ _____ all of them in the school hall and that's how we ⁶ _____ The One Hundred.'

Mr Browning, Molly's music teacher, ⁷ _____ them, and a month ago The One Hundred ⁸ _____ a concert for charity. They ⁹ _____ £1,675!

Well done, Molly!

6 Write questions about Molly from Exercise 5. Then ask and answer with your partner.

1 what kind of music / Molly / want / to play?
What kind of music did Molly want to play?

2 where / she / post / the ad?
....

3 how many students / answer / the ad?
....

4 where / Molly / meet / them?
....

5 who / support / The One Hundred?
....

6 how much money / they / make?
....

A Extension exercises

1 Match the questions with the answers to complete the interview with Darcy D.

An interview with Darcy D!
by Sue Davies and Kylie Winston

Sue: Hi, Darcy! Can we ask you some questions?

Darcy: Sure. What do you want to know?

Kylie: When you were at school, [1] *d*

Darcy: All kinds: pop, jazz, hip hop, blues ...

Sue: [2] ....

Darcy: I played the piano. I was terrible but my brother was brilliant!

Kylie: [3] ....

Darcy: When I was sixteen. I sang in a band with my brother and his friends.

Sue: [4] ....

Darcy: My brother started it. It was called The Fleas.

Kylie: The year 2010 was very special for you. [5] ....

Darcy: My brother posted a video of me on YouTube. People loved it and I became famous! Then I made four albums.

Sue: [6] ....

Darcy: My favourite was *Moonlighting*.

Kylie: Thanks for talking to us, Darcy, and good luck with your next album!

a Which album was your favourite?
b Who started the band?
c What instruments did you play?
d what kind of music did you like?
e What happened?
f When did you start singing?

2 Choose the correct answers.

Sue and Kylie posted the interview and asked readers to send questions to Darcy.

1 Which of your albums sold the most copies last year?
   a I think it was *Blue Monday*.
   b It sold 47,000 copies.
   c *Moonlighting* is my favourite album.

2 What charities do you support?
   a Singers support a lot of charities.
   b Charities need a lot of money.
   c A small charity for children in Africa.

3 Who gave the band its name, The Fleas?
   a In 2008.
   b Paul, a friend of my brother's.
   c I liked it but my brother didn't.

4 Where was your last concert?
   a It was in 2008.
   b London or Birmingham. I don't remember.
   c I want to sing in New York.

5 What do your parents think of your music?
   a They enjoy it but they prefer jazz.
   b My dad wanted me to be a doctor.
   c My mum wanted to be a singer, too.

About you

3 Find a photo of your favourite singer. Then answer the questions.

1 Who is your favourite singer?
....

2 How old is he/she?
....

3 Who writes his/her songs?
....

4 Which of his/her albums sold the most copies?
....

5 Does he/she support any charities?
....

B Foundation exercises

Vocabulary: Transport

1 Write the words.

1 ....plane............

2 ....

3 ....

4 ....

5 ....

6 ....

7 ....

Grammar: Prepositions with means of transport

2 Choose the correct words.

1 I go to school **by** / on train.
2 My sister doesn't *walk / cycle* to school. She goes by bike.
3 He goes to school *by / on* Underground.
4 They went to the United States *by / on* plane.
5 We don't go to school by *car / cycle*.
6 Do you and your brother always cycle *by / to* school?

Memory check: Dates and times

3 Complete the sentences.

1 It's 3.35.
   It's three thirty-......*five*.......

2 It's 30th September.
   It's the thirtieth .... September.

3 It's 7 o'clock.
   It's .... o'clock.

4 It's 22nd November.
   It's the ....-second of November.

5 It's 6.30.
   It's half .... six.

6 It's 1st January.
   It's the .... of January.

7 It's 9.45.
   It's quarter .... ten.

8 It's 30th March.
   It's the .... of March.

Vocabulary: Directions

4 Complete the directions.

| ~~along~~ | on | past | right | the | turn |

It's easy to get to my house. Get off the bus at the stop in Valley Road. Then walk ¹ ...*along*.... Valley Road. Don't ² .... left at the park – that goes to the town centre. Walk ³ .... it. Turn ⁴ .... at the supermarket. Then go straight ⁵ .... My house is on ⁶ .... left.

About you

5 Answer the questions about you.

1 What date is your birthday?

   ....

2 What date is your mum's birthday?

   ....

3 What date is your dad's birthday?

   ....

4 What date is your best friend's birthday?

   ....

5 How do you go to school?

   ....

B Activation exercises

Vocabulary: Transport

1 Read the clues and write the words for types of transport.

What am I?

1 My first letter is in *brother* but not in *mother*.
My second letter is in *cup* but not in *cap*.
My third letter is in *star* but not in *art*.
I'm a ....

2 My first letter is in *nice* but not in *nine*.
My second letter is in *pool* but not in *pull*.
My third letter is in *please* but not in *sleep*.
My fourth letter is in *cold* but not in *doll*.
My fifth letter is in *house* but not in *mouse*.
I'm a ....

3 My first letter is in *bike* but not in *kite*.
My second letter is in *orange* but not in *garden*.
My third letter is in *watch* but not in *which*.
My fourth letter is in *water* but not in *warmer*.
I'm a ....

2 Write puzzles like the ones in Exercise 1 for four types of transport.

What am I?

1 My first ....
....
....
....

2 ....
....
....
....

3 ....
....
....
....

4 ....
....
....
....

Grammar: Prepositions with means of transport

3 Complete the sentences. There are two extra words.

~~by~~ by car cycle train Underground walk

We asked three pupils how they get to school. This is what they said.

I usually go to school
¹ ....*by*........... bus in the winter but I often walk there in the summer.

I usually walk to school but I sometimes ² .... In the winter I go by ³ ....
My mum drives me.

My school is near the centre of town and I usually go there
⁴ .... Underground. My friends meet me at the station and then we ⁵ .... to school.

4 Look at the table and complete the text.

Survey: How do pupils in Bramley get to school?

	🚌	Ⓤ	🚲	🚶	🚗
Summer	5	1	6	12	7
Winter	12	3	1	5	10

In the summer five children go to school
¹ ....*by bus*.... . Only one child goes ² ....
Six children ³ .... to school and twelve
⁴ .... Seven children go to school
⁵ ....

In the winter things are different. Twelve children go to school ⁶ .... Three go ⁷ ....
Only one child ⁸ .... and five children
⁹ .... Ten children go ¹⁰ ....

44

Vocabulary: Directions

5 **Match the sentence halves.**

1 Walk along
2 Don't turn left. Go
3 My house is on
4 Turn right
5 Walk past

a at the supermarket.
b straight on.
c the park.
d the right.
e the street.

6 (3 35) **Listen to Maria giving directions to Dario and draw the route on the map.**

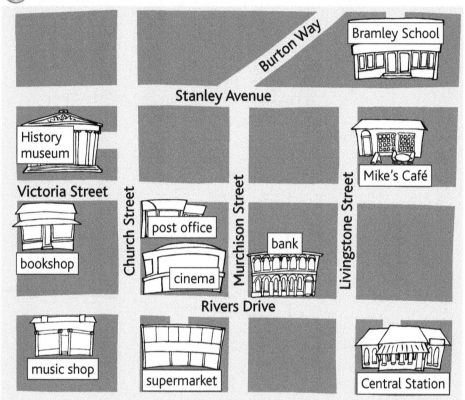

7 **Look at the map in Exercise 6 and complete Maria's directions to her friends.**

1 'Hi, Maria! I'm at the station. How do I get to the bookshop?'

'Hi, George! It's easy. Walk along ¹ _Rivers Drive_. Turn ² .... at the cinema.
Go along Church Street and turn left into ³ .... Go ⁴ .... on. The bookshop
is on the ⁵ ....'

2 'Hey, Maria! I'm at the music shop. Where's Mike's Café?'

'Go along Rivers Drive, ⁶ .... the cinema and the bank, and turn ⁷ .... into
Livingstone Street. Go straight on for about two minutes. Mike's Café is on the ⁸ ....'

3 'We're at school and we need to go to the supermarket. Where is it?'

'Go left for a few metres. Then turn ⁹ .... again into Burton Way. Walk ¹⁰ ....
Murchison Street and turn right into Rivers Drive. You can't miss the supermarket – it's big!'

B Extension exercises

1 **Read the invitation and look at the map. Then complete the dialogue.**

50 years!

George and *Carole Evans* invite all the members of their family and their dear friends to their fiftieth wedding anniversary party!

Saturday 23rd September, 7.30 p.m.
31 Charlton Road, Middlington
Phone: 786520

Jess: Hi, Andy. We need your help.

Andy: Sure. What is it?

Jess: We can't find the invitation to your grandparents' party. Is it on Saturday or Sunday?

Andy: [1] _Saturday_ .

Jess: What date is it?

Andy: The [2] .... of September.

Jess: What time?

Andy: Let me see ... At [3] .... seven.

Jess: I remember their address: 31 Charlton Road. But how can we get there?

Andy: Well, you can come [4] .... car or you can take the Underground to the nearest station. Then you can walk. It isn't far.

Jess: Oh, the Underground! Dad hates driving. Can you give me directions?

Andy: You come out of the Underground, turn [5] .... and then [6] .... again into Millington Road. Go [7] .... on for about ten minutes and then [8] .... left into Charlton Road. Walk [9] .... the post office and the park. My grandparents' house is on the [10] ....

2 **Look at the map in Exercise 1 and write directions to George and Carole's party.**

1 from the Rex Cinema
Come out of the cinema and turn right. ....
....

2 from Hugo's music shop
Come out of the music shop and walk along ....
....

3 from the sports centre
Come out of the entrance and ....
....

About you

3 **Answer the questions about you.**

1 How do you get to school?
....

2 How do you get to your best friend's house?
....

3 How do you get to the supermarket from your house?
....

4 How does your best friend go to school?
....

Speaking: Ask for directions

1 **Write the words in the correct order.**

1 A: I | to | from | how | get | do | here?
the Science Museum

How do I get to the Science Museum from here?

B: to take | the number 36 bus. | need | you

....

2 A: you | tell | can | the post office? | me | to
the way

....

B: it's | the street. | at | of | the end

....

3 A: the train station? | do | how | I | to | get

....

B: I'm not sure. | that | think | I | way. | it's

....

4 A: for | looking | the Odeon Cinema. | I'm

....

B: from | walk | a bit far | to | it's | here.

....

2 **Complete the dialogues.**

for	~~me~~	need	on	sure	thanks	to
walk	way	welcome				

Luke: Excuse [1] ......*me*....... . How do I get
[2] .... the post office?

Woman: It's a bit far to [3] .... from here. You
[4] .... to take the number 11 bus. The
bus station is down the street, [5] ....
the right.

Luke: Thank you very much.

Woman: You're [6] ....

Emma: Excuse me, sir. I'm looking [7] .... a
bookshop called Readers' Corner. Can you
tell me the way?

Man: I'm not [8] .... I think it's that
[9] ...., down Wesley Street.

Emma: [10] .... a lot.

Writing: Written directions

3 **Complete the sentences with *when* or *then*.**

1 .....*When*..... you arrive at the supermarket, turn left
into Wood Street.

2 Walk past the bank. .... turn right.

3 Walk past the museum. .... you arrive at
the cinema, don't turn left. Turn right.

4 First, take the Underground to Oxford Circus.
.... walk down Oxford Street and turn left
at Wardour Street.

Your turn

4 **You are in a talent competition at the Town
Hall. Write an email to give directions to your
best friend. Use the notes to help you.**

Hi ....,

I'm so happy you can come to the talent
competition with me and my parents! I know
your mum doesn't want to drive you there,
so here are directions to the Town Hall.

First, you ....
....

When you get to the station, ...
....
....

Get off the bus, then ....
and ....
.... Then ....
....
....

The Town Hall ....

I can't wait to see you!

Love,

....

– train to town
– number 6 bus to
  Hillside Road
– walk past bank and café
– right into Main Street
– Town Hall: left

Check

1 **Choose the correct answers to complete the quiz.**

Do our quiz and win a fantastic prize!

1 ...... city did The Beatles come from, London or Liverpool?

2 Who ...... the album *21*?

3 Did Elvis Presley play the ......?

4 When did Leona Lewis ...... *The X Factor*?

5 Did Mozart write ...... music?

6 ...... started the rock band Led Zeppelin?

7 ...... kind of music did Louis Armstrong play?

Answers
1 Liverpool **2** Adele **3** Yes, he did. **4** in 2006
5 Yes, he did. **6** Jimmy Page **7** Jazz

1	**a**	How	**ⓑ**	Which	**c**	Who
2	**a**	make	**b**	did make	**c**	made
3	**a**	piano	**b**	classical	**c**	rock
4	**a**	win	**b**	wins	**c**	won
5	**a**	coach	**b**	drums	**c**	classical
6	**a**	How	**b**	Who	**c**	Where
7	**a**	What	**b**	When	**c**	Who

Score: .... /6

2 **Complete the dialogue.**

> at six o'clock   at the end of the street   by car   ~~Can you come?~~   How do I get
> I can cycle   It's a bit far   Then turn right   When you arrive   You need to take

Leila: Hi, Sophie! I'm playing the piano in a school concert on Friday.
¹ *Can you come?* ....

Sophie: Yes, of course! I want to hear you! What time is the concert?

Leila: It's ² ....

Sophie: ³ .... to your school?

Leila: Can you come ⁴ ....?

Sophie: No, I can't. Mum works and she comes home late on Fridays.
But ⁵ ....

Leila: ⁶ .... to cycle from your house.
⁷ .... the Underground.
⁸ .... at the station, walk along
Waverley Street. ⁹ .... at the café.
My school is ¹⁰ ....

Sophie: Great, thanks! See you on Friday!

Score: .... /9

My score is ....!

48

5 Things I like

A Foundation exercises

Vocabulary: Geographical features

1 Write the words.

| beach | ~~forest~~ | hill | island | lake | mountain | rainforest | river | sea | volcano |

1 ....._forest_.....   2 ....   3 ....   4 ....

5 ....   6 ....   7 ....

8 ....   9 ....   10 ....

Grammar: Comparative and superlative of short adjectives

2 Complete the table.

Adjective	Comparative	Superlative
hot	¹ ....._hotter_.....	the hottest
large	larger	² ....
long	³	the longest
⁴	nicer	the nicest
deep	⁵	⁶ ....
⁷	bigger	⁸ ....

3 Complete the sentences with the comparative and the superlative of the adjectives.

1 Mount Olympus is high. Mont Blanc is _higher than_ Mount Olympus. Mount Everest is _the highest_.

2 The swimming pool is deep. The lake is .... the swimming pool. The sea is ....

3 China is big. Canada is .... China. Russia is ....

4 30°C is hot. 35°C is .... 30°C. 40°C is ....

5 Liechtenstein is small. Monaco is .... Liechtenstein. Vatican City is ....

6 Moscow is large. Cairo is .... Moscow. Tokyo is ....

A Activation exercises

Vocabulary: Geographical features

1 Complete the crossword.

Across

5 There is a lot of water in this but you can't drink it! People can swim and fish in it, and they can also travel on it.

7 It has got a lot of trees.

9 There is a lot of water in it. People can swim and fish in it.

10 They are high but other places are higher!

Down

1 Greece has got a lot of these. There is water all around them.

2 It is hot and it rains a lot here. It has got huge trees.

3 They are very high places. Some have got snow at the top.

4 This is a very dangerous mountain!

6 People sit and play on it. It's next to the sea.

8 It is long and it has got a lot of water.

Crossword grid with numbered cells 1–10. Down clue 1 spells: i s l a n d s

2 Complete the fact file with words from Exercise 1.

Geography fact file

1 Copacabana *Beach* is in Brazil and Waikiki *Beach* is in Hawaii.

2 The Black .... is in Germany but it isn't really black!

3 Majorca, Sicily and Crete are ....

4 Lake Geneva and Loch Ness are European ....

5 Everest, Kilimanjaro and Olympus are famous ....

6 The Amazon .... has got lots of animals and beautiful birds.

7 The Nile, the Thames and the Ebro are famous ....

8 The Mediterranean and the Caribbean are ....

9 Etna is a famous .... in Italy.

Grammar: Comparative and superlative of short adjectives

3 Match the sentence halves.

1 Scotland is a cold country
2 Lake Geneva is deep
3 The hills are high
4 Brazil is a hot country
5 The Thames is a long river
6 Switzerland is a small country

a but Andorra is smaller.
b but Ethiopia is hotter.
c but Greenland is colder.
d but the Mississippi is longer.
e but the mountains are higher.
f but the Mediterranean Sea is deeper.

4 Write sentences with the comparative of the adjectives.

1 Luke / old / Emma   *Luke is older than Emma.*

2 Emma / young / Sophie   ....

3 Sophie's hair / long / Emma's hair   ....

4 Luke / short / Seb   ....

5 Seb's house / big / Luke's house   ....

5 Complete the fact file with the superlative of the adjectives.

Fact file: Russia

- Russia is [1] _the largest_ (large) country in the world.
- It has one of [2] _____ (cold) climates in the world. [3] _____ (hot) part of Russia is near the Black Sea.
- Moscow is the capital of Russia and it is also [4] _____ (big) city in the country. More than 11,500,000 people live there.
- The Volga is [5] _____ (long) river in Europe. It is 3,692 km long.
- Mount Elbrus is [6] _____ (high) mountain in Europe. It is 5,642 m high.
- Lake Baikal is [7] _____ (old) lake in the world – 25,000,000 years old! It is also [8] _____ (deep) lake in the world.

Black Sea
Moscow
the Volga
Lake Baikal
Mount Elbrus

6 Choose the correct words.

1 Is Athens older / the oldest city in Greece?
2 Barcelona is bigger / the biggest than Valencia but Madrid is bigger / the biggest city in Spain.
3 The River Seine is longer / the longest than the River Garonne but it isn't longer / the longest river in France.
4 Portugal is hotter / the hottest than England.
5 Loch Lomond is a larger / the largest lake than Loch Ness but Loch Ness is deeper / the deepest.
6 Mauna Kea in Hawaii is higher / the highest volcano in the world.

English today

7 Complete the dialogue.

| ~~for~~ | huge | map | miss | silly | think |

Luke: What are you doing, Emma?
Emma: A Geography project about Russia. I'm looking [1] _for_ the Volga River on the [2] _____ but I can't find it.
Luke: Really? It's [3] _____! You can't [4] _____ it. Here it is.
Emma: Oh! Now I see it. [5] _____ me! Is it the longest river in the country?
Luke: I [6] _____ so. In fact, it's the longest river in Europe.

About you

8 Answer the questions about you.

1 Who is the oldest member of your family?
The oldest member of my family is _____
2 Who is the youngest member of your family?
_____
3 Who is the shortest member of your family?
_____
4 Who is older: you or your best friend?
_____
5 Who is taller: you or your best friend?
_____
6 Who has got longer hair: you or your best friend?
_____

A Extension exercises

1 Read the texts and write *Chun* (*C*), *Mario* (*M*) or *Jéssica* (*J*).

Hi! I'm Chun and Canada's my favourite country! The winter here is very cold and it snows a lot but it doesn't matter. Canada's so beautiful and it's got everything: huge forests and lakes, and high mountains. There are also some great cities. I come from Ottawa, the country's capital. It isn't the biggest city in the country but it's one of the cleanest in the world.

My name's Mario and I'm Italian. I come from Siracusa, a very old Sicilian city with a rich history. Sicily is the largest island in Italy. It's got beautiful hills and fantastic beaches. The weather is also great and in the summer we go swimming every day in the blue Mediterranean Sea. And, of course, Sicily has got a famous volcano: Mount Etna, the highest active volcano in Europe.

I'm Jéssica and I'm Brazilian. Brazilians are the friendliest people in the world and Brazil is an amazing country! It's got the world's largest rainforest, with huge trees and millions of animals and plants, the Amazon River, great beaches – and the best football in the world! I come from Rio de Janeiro. It isn't the capital – that's Brasilia – but it's the second largest city in Brazil and one of the most interesting cities in the world.

1 This person's country has got a famous volcano. ....*M*....

2 This person comes from the capital of the country. ....

3 This person talks about his/her country's weather. .... and ....

4 This person says his/her country is famous for a sport. ....

5 This person's country has got a lot of trees. .... and ....

6 This person talks about his/her country's past. ....

2 Look at the table and choose the correct answers.

Canada	Italy	Brazil
Mount Logan: 5,959 metres high	Mont Blanc: 4,810 metres high	Pico da Neblina: 2,994 metres high
Mackenzie River: 1,738 kilometres long	River Po: 652 kilometres long	Amazon River: 6,400 kilometres long*
Baffin Island: 507,451 square kilometres	Sicily: 25,711 square kilometres	Marajó: 40,100 square kilometres

*This is the total length of the Amazon, from its origin in Peru to the Atlantic Ocean.

1 Which country has the highest mountain?
  (a) Canada has the highest mountain.
  b Mount Logan is higher.
  c Italy has the highest mountain.

2 Which mountain is higher than Mont Blanc?
  a No mountain is higher.
  b Mount Logan
  c Pico da Neblina

3 Which country has the shortest river?
  a the River Po
  b Italy
  c Canada

4 Which river is the longest?
  a The Amazon is longer than the Mackenzie River.
  b the Mackenzie River
  c the Amazon

5 Which island is smaller than Marajó?
  a Baffin island is bigger than Sicily.
  b Sicily
  c Baffin Island

6 Which island is the biggest?
  a Marajó
  b Sicily
  c Baffin Island

About you

3 Write about your favourite country. Use Exercise 1 and these ideas to help you.

- What has it got? (e.g. beaches, forests, hills, islands, lakes, mountains, rivers)
- What is the capital city? What is it like?

B Foundation exercises

5

Vocabulary: Adjectives (2)

1 Find and write ten adjectives.

B	A	C	F	S	A	F	E	E	Q	C
O	E	G	R	A	C	A	L	X	S	F
R	I	U	I	C	W	D	A	P	A	O
I	N	T	E	L	L	I	G	E	N	T
N	A	A	N	E	A	R	R	N	A	A
G	U	A	D	A	Z	T	I	S	O	L
A	G	B	L	N	Y	Y	B	I	A	T
D	L	M	Y	A	E	N	V	V	E	J
P	Y	A	E	H	G	C	H	E	A	P

1 .... *safe* ....
2 ....
3 ....
4 ....
5 ....
6 ....
7 ....
8 ....
9 ....
10 ....

2 Choose the adjectives with the opposite meaning.

1 My cat isn't ugly. It's *dirty / beautiful.*
2 The book wasn't interesting. It was *boring / energetic.*
3 That car isn't cheap. It's *interesting / expensive.*

4 This animal isn't dangerous. It's *intelligent / safe.*
5 The plate isn't dirty. It's *clean / friendly.*
6 Those children aren't energetic. They're *lazy / boring.*

Grammar: Comparative and superlative of long and irregular adjectives

3 Write the adjectives in the correct bags.

> ~~energetic~~   worse   the most dangerous   good   the most expensive   ~~more energetic~~   the best   bad
> dangerous   expensive   more dangerous   the worst   ~~the most energetic~~   better   more expensive

Adjectives

energetic

Comparative adjectives

more energetic

Superlative adjectives

the most energetic

About you

4 Answer the questions about you.

1 Is your town or city beautiful? — *Yes, it is. / No, it isn't.*
2 Is your town or city safe? — *Yes, it is. / No, it isn't.*
3 Has your town or city got interesting places? — *Yes, it has. / No, it hasn't.*
4 Has your town or city got expensive shops? — *Yes, it has. / No, it hasn't.*

53

B Activation exercises

Vocabulary: Adjectives (2)

1 Write the opposites to complete the puzzle. Then find the mystery word and complete the sentence.

1 interesting
2 lazy
3 dirty
4 safe
5 clean
6 cheap
7 dangerous
8 beautiful
9 energetic

1	b o r i n g

My country is the most .... country in the world!

2 Complete the sentences.

beautiful	boring	cheap	dangerous	energetic	expensive	~~friendly~~	intelligent

1 He's got lots of friends. He's a ...._friendly_.... person.
2 The children play all day. They're very ....
3 These jeans are only £10. They're ....
4 She's good at Maths and Science and she knows a lot of things. She's ....

5 I love looking at the sea. It's so .... !
6 That car is £150,000! That's .... !
7 I didn't like the film. It was ....
8 Don't go near the snake! It's .... !

Grammar: Comparative and superlative of long and irregular adjectives

3 Choose the correct words.

Brazil trip

1 Monday 15th

It's fantastic to be here in Brazil! It's a [beautiful]/ more beautiful country and I think it's [2]better/the best country in the world! Today we're in Rio de Janeiro. I love it because it's [3]more interesting/the most interesting than Brasilia, the capital. Mum gets cross when I say this because she comes from Brasilia!

2 Saturday 20th

We went to the rainforest on Thursday and it was [4]more amazing/the most amazing time of my life! It's a [5]dangerous/more dangerous place but Dad says some cities are [6]more dangerous/the most dangerous than the rainforest! We saw lots of animals: monkeys, snakes and macaws. I want a macaw for a pet because they're so [7]intelligent/more intelligent!

3 Monday 22nd

Today we're back in Rio and we're visiting my cousin, Fabio. He's got a pet chinchilla! He thinks chinchillas are [8]better/the best pets in the world because they're very [9]energetic/more energetic and [10]clean/cleaner than most other pets. I still think macaws are better. Tomorrow Fabio is taking me to the Copacabana Beach, [11]popular/the most popular beach in Rio. Fantastic!

Seb

4 Match the days in Seb's blog in Exercise 3 with the photos. There is one extra photo.

5 Write about the extra photo in Exercise 4. Use the notes to help you.

weather: sunny and hot – a lot hotter than England!

beach: beautiful, most popular in Rio

what we did: went swimming, played football – Fabio better than me, more energetic

My blog... Wednesday 24th

Yesterday we went to the Copacabana Beach with my cousin Fabio. The weather was ....

6 Read Seb's blog in Exercise 3 and answer the questions.

1 Which is Seb's favourite country?
Seb's favourite country is Brazil.
2 Which city does Seb prefer: Rio de Janeiro or Brasilia?

3 Where is Seb's mum from?

4 Where did Seb go on Thursday?

5 What does Seb's dad say about the rainforest?

6 Why does Seb want a macaw for a pet?

7 Why does Fabio think chinchillas are the best pets?

8 Where are Fabio and Seb going to go on Tuesday 23rd?

B Extension exercises

1 Read the text and complete the star chart.

Great cats: which one is best for you?

	British shorthair	Burmese	Persian
energetic	★★	★★★	★
friendly			
intelligent			
clean			

Some cats are energetic and some cats sleep all day. What kind of cat do you prefer?

Persian cats are often a bit lazy! The British shorthair cat is more energetic than the Persian. The Burmese is the most energetic.

Do you want a friendly cat? Remember: not all cats like people!

The most friendly cat is the Burmese. The Persian is more friendly than the British shorthair.

Do you want an intelligent cat?

The British shorthair is more intelligent than the Persian cat. The Burmese is the most intelligent cat but it doesn't always listen to you!

Do you want a clean cat?

All cats are clean! The British shorthair is the cleanest but the Burmese is cleaner than the Persian. The Persian cat has a long coat – it's hard work to clean it!

2 Complete the dialogue with the correct form of the adjectives.

Emma: This is a fantastic website – look at these beautiful cats!

Sophie: Oh, I love cats! This Persian is [1] _the most beautiful_ (beautiful) cat here; and it's got
[2] .... (big) eyes of all.

Emma: Well, maybe you're right but I don't think it's very [3] .... (intelligent). The Burmese and the English shorthair are [4] .... (intelligent). And the Burmese cat is [5] .... (friendly) than the Persian.

Sophie: Oh! Here's a website about fish! Look at the colours of those fish!

Emma: Wow! They're [6] .... (amazing)! But I prefer dogs. I want a bulldog for my birthday.

Sophie: Good idea! My mum thinks bulldogs are [7] .... (ugly) but I think they're [8] .... (cool) dogs in the world!

About you

3 Look at the cats in Exercise 1. Which cat do you like? Why?

....

....

....

....

C Foundation exercises

Vocabulary: Outdoor equipment

1 Complete the words for outdoor equipment.

3 w....te...p...oof j....... .....et

4 h....k....n.... b.......ts

2 r....c...s....ck

1 te....n...t

6 m....p

5 G....S w....... .....ch

8 tr....... .....ksu....t

7 t....r....h

9 sl....... .....ing ba....

10 t....ai..... ....rs

Memory check: Money

2 Match.

1	50p	a	five pounds ninety-nine
2	29p	b	fifty pence
3	£1	c	one pound
4	£2.90	d	sixteen pounds forty
5	£5.99	e	twenty-nine pence
6	£16.40	f	two pounds ninety
7	£250	g	two hundred and fifty pounds

Grammar: Infinitive of purpose; Object pronoun: one/ones

3 Complete the sentences with the correct verb forms.

carry	~~find~~	sleep	tell	walk

1 Dad used his GPS watch ....*to find*.... the way to the camp.
2 We had a tent .... in at night.
3 I had a rucksack .... all my things.
4 My sister wore hiking boots .... in the mountains.
5 I phoned Mum .... her about our trip.

4 Choose the correct words.

1 **A:** I need some new trainers.
   B: Those *one* / *ones* over there are nice.
2 **A:** How many tracksuits have you got?
   B: I've got two: a blue *one* / *ones* and a black *one* / *ones*.
3 **A:** Take your umbrella to school with you today.
   B: Why do I need *one* / *ones*?
4 **A:** Macaw parrots are beautiful birds.
   B: Yes. The red and blue *one* / *ones* are my favourites.
5 **A:** I'd like a pet but not a dog or cat.
   B: A rat is a good *one* / *ones*.

C Activation exercises

Vocabulary: Outdoor equipment

1 Match the sentences with the outdoor equipment.

1 You wear it. It's warm.   a GPS watch
2 You sleep in it.   b hiking boots
3 You wear it when it rains.   c rucksack
4 You use it when you want to see at night.   d tent
5 You need it to find your way.   e torch
6 You put things in it and carry it.   f tracksuit
7 You wear these on your feet to walk in the mountains.   g waterproof jacket

2 3/36 Listen to Sophie talking to her mum and tick (✓) the things Sophie has got.

1 GPS watch ☐   6 tent   ☐
2 hiking boots ☐   7 torch   ☐
3 map ☐   8 tracksuit   ☐
4 rucksack ☐   9 trainers   ☐
5 sleeping bag ☐   10 waterproof jacket ☐

Memory check: Money

3 Look at the prices and complete the dialogues.

1

£10.99
£6.99

A: How much was the hat?
B: *Ten pounds ninety-nine.*.......................................
A: How much is it now?
B: ....

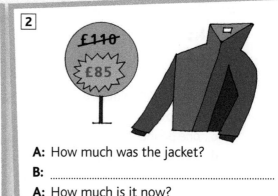

2

£110
£85

A: How much was the jacket?
B: ....
A: How much is it now?
B: ....

3

£50
£39.50

A: How much were the hiking boots?
B: ....
A: How much are they now?
B: ....

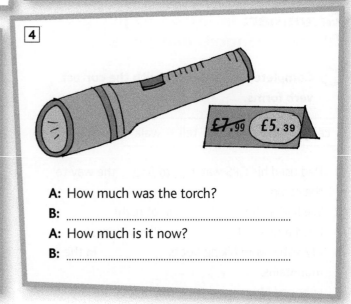

4

£7.99 £5.39

A: How much was the torch?
B: ....
A: How much is it now?
B: ....

Grammar: Infinitive of purpose; Object pronoun: *one/ones*

4 Write the words in the correct order.

1 [a GPS watch] [to] [she] [her way] [find] [needs]

   She needs a GPS watch to find her way.

2 [went] [buy] [to] [the supermarket] [to] [I] [some milk]

   ....

3 [to] [he] [the news] [phoned] [me] [tell] [me]

   ....

4 [find] [are] [information] [surfing] [they] [to] [the Internet]

   ....

5 [we] [the map] [our way] [to] [looked at] [find]

   ....

6 [some money] [buy] [gave] [me] [to] [she] [a book]

   ....

5 Complete the text with the correct verb forms.

~~buy~~ find get keep see walk

Dave's blog

●●●●●●●●●●●●●●●●●●●●●●●●

My family and I went camping last weekend. On Friday afternoon Mum took me to town
¹ __to buy__ a new sleeping bag. I also wanted a GPS watch. I think we need one
² .... our way but Mum says they're very expensive. Then we went home
³ .... our equipment ready. We put waterproof jackets in our rucksacks
⁴ .... warm and dry – it often rains in England! We also took our hiking boots
⁵ .... in the hills. We forgot to take a torch with us and we needed it ⁶ ....
in the dark but, fortunately, there was a moon. We had a great time!

6 Complete the dialogues with *one* or *ones*.

1 **Mum:** I saw three dresses I liked: a black ...*one*... and two blue ....

   Sophie: Which .... did you buy?

   Mum: The black ....

2 **Emma:** Which are your trainers, Luke?

   Luke: Those .... The other .... are Seb's.

3 **Seb:** Did you see any good films last weekend?

   Luke: Yes, I saw a good .... on TV.

4 **Dad:** Where are the maps, Seb?

   Seb: Which ....?

   Dad: Well, I'm looking for a map of Brighton.

   Seb: I don't know but there's .... over there.

English today

7 Put the dialogue in the correct order.

Emma! It's £65! That's far too expensive!	....
A map.	....
First, I need a new tracksuit.	....
Oh, Mum! They're old! Here, have a look. I like this black and white one.	....
Good idea. A map is useful.	....
OK, Emma. What do you need?	....
Mum, I need some things for the school trip.	_1_
What about this one? It's only £45.	....
Why do you need a new one? You've got three tracksuits at home.	....
Oh, and I need one more thing ...	_11_
Well, OK. What else do you need?	....

C Extension exercises

1 Complete the questions and answers about camping. Write one or two words in each gap.

Q: What equipment do I need to take with me?

A: Well, you need a [1] _tent_ but you don't need a big [2] .... because there are small tents for two people. These are good because you can use them with a friend.

Q: What kind of sleeping bag do I need to take with me?

A: A warm [3] ....! Some sleeping bags are waterproof. Those are the best.

Q: Do I need a GPS watch?

A: A GPS watch can help you to [4] .... your way. But these watches can be expensive. Of course, a [5] .... is useful, and it's cheaper.

Q: Do I need hiking boots? Can't I wear [6] ....?

A: You [7] .... hiking boots [8] .... in the mountains. They're better than trainers because they're stronger.

Q: Why do I need to take a [9] ....? It's summer!

A: You need [10] .... to keep dry and warm. The weather in the mountains changes all the time and it often rains.

Q: Why do I need to take a [11] ....?

A: You need one to see at night!

2 Read the questions and answers in Exercise 1 and answer the questions.

1 What equipment do people ask about?

Tents, sleeping bags, GPS watches, maps, hiking boots, trainers, waterproof jackets and torches.

2 Why don't you need a big tent?

....

....

3 What kind of sleeping bags are the best?

....

....

4 What equipment do you need to help you to find your way?

....

....

5 Why are hiking boots better than trainers when you are in the mountains?

....

....

About you

3 You are going camping. Write sentences about the outdoor equipment you need. Use your own ideas and Exercises 1 and 2 to help you.

Our class is going camping next week.
I need to take some good outdoor equipment.
I need ....

....

....

....

....

....

....

....

....

Speaking: Buy a present

1 **Write the words in the correct order.**

1 | Macaw parrot? | how | for | about | her | a new cage |

How about a new cage for her Macaw parrot?

2 | get | Lily | book | parrots. | let's | about | this |

....

3 | expensive! | too | far | that's |

....

4 | than | the book | the cage. | cheaper | is |

....

5 | the | cage | or | do you | black one? | prefer – | which | the | gold one |

....

2 **Complete the dialogue with the sentences in Exercise 1.**

Fred and Katie are trying to choose a birthday present for their cousin Lily.

Katie: Lily loves animals.

Fred: Those cages over there are awesome! [1] *How about a new cage for her Macaw parrot?*

Katie: They're beautiful! [2] ....

Fred: The gold one. Oh!

Katie: What's wrong?

Fred: It's £99! [3] ....

Katie: And we've only got £30.

Fred: I know! [4] ....

Katie: Good idea! [5] ....

Your turn

3 **You and a friend are buying a birthday present for another friend. Write the dialogue. Use Exercise 1 to help you.**

You: .... loves ....

...............: Those .... are awesome!

You: ....

...............: ....

You: ....

...............: ....

You: ....

Writing: Write a review

4 **Complete the ideas for a review.**

bigger and heavier than my old camera
four stars   more pixels than other cameras
~~Pandora MXR digital camera~~
present for my birthday   quite expensive – £120
takes fantastic photos

1 Topic: ....._Pandora MXR digital camera_.....
2 How/When I got it: ....
....
3 Compare with other cameras: ....
....
4 What I like: ....
....
5 What I don't like: ....
....
6 Price: ....
....
7 Rating: ....
....

5 **Write a review for the Pandora MXR. Use the ideas in Exercise 4 to help you.**

The Pandora MXR is a digital camera.
I got it ....
It's ....
It has ....
and it takes ....
....
There is only one problem: ....
....

Check

1 **Choose the correct answers to complete the email.**

Hi Lulu,

Thanks for your email! I'm having ¹ .... holiday of my life! Brazil is the ² .... country in the world! It's far ³ .... and hotter ⁴ .... England, of course! My brother Jeremy and I love the ⁵ .... and we go swimming every day.

Two weeks ago, we visited Brasilia – that's the capital of Brazil. It's ⁶ .... city but I think Rio is ⁷ .... interesting. Last week, we took a trip to the ⁸ .... The trees were ⁹ ....! It rained a lot but we had a great time and I saw Macaw parrots. They're ¹⁰ .... beautiful birds in the world.

The people here are great, too. Brazilians are very ¹¹ ....

How is your holiday? Write soon.

Valerie

	a	**b**	**c**
1	amazing	more amazing	ⓒ the most amazing
2	good	better	best
3	big	bigger	biggest
4	that	than	from
5	beaches	hills	forests
6	an interesting	more interesting	the most interesting
7	an	more	most
8	sea	island	rainforest
9	huge	energetic	cheap
10	more	most	the most
11	expensive	friendly	lazy

Score: .... /10

2 **Choose the correct answers.**

1 Where's Russia on the map?
ⓐ You can't miss it.   **b** Silly me!   **c** That's far too dangerous.

2 Is the Zambezi River in Africa?
a It's in the forest.   **b** Silly me!   **c** I think so.

3 Have you got everything?
a I need one more thing.   **b** It's very expensive.   **c** I prefer that one.

4 Let's get Mum this mountain bike for her birthday.
a Have a look.   **b** It's far too expensive!   **c** I think so.

5 Which do you prefer?
a I think so.   **b** They're too dangerous.   **c** The black one.

6 Why do you need a map?
a I miss the beaches.   **b** To find my way.   **c** I prefer a GPS watch.

Score: .... /5

My score is ....!

6 Day by day

A Foundation exercises

Vocabulary: Clothes; Adjectives to describe clothes

1 Write the words.

| belt | dress | hat | jacket | jeans | jumper | leggings | scarf | shirt | shoes |
| shorts | skirt | socks | suit | ~~sweatshirt~~ | tie | trousers | T-shirt |

1 ....sweatshirt....

2 ....

3 ....

4 ....

5 ....

6 ....

7 ....

8 ....

9 ....

10 ....

11 ....

12 ....

13 ....

14 ....

15 ....

16 ....

17 ....

18 ....

2 Complete the adjectives to describe clothes.

1 b_i_g
2 ...ld
3 sh......t
4 sty.........h
5 b......gy
6 l......g
7 s...a...t
8 ......ght
9 c.........al
10 ......d-f...s.........ed
11 ...ew
12 s......ll

Grammar: *too* + adjective; Adjective + *enough*

3 Choose the correct words.

1 This shirt is (too)/ enough small. I need a bigger one.
2 This coffee is too / enough hot. I can't drink it.
3 Jeans aren't smart too / enough for the party. Wear your skirt.
4 I can't watch the film. It's too / enough scary.
5 We didn't watch the film last night. It wasn't interesting too / enough.
6 The boy can't go to school. He isn't old too / enough.
7 I can't buy this camera! It's too / enough expensive.
8 Don't swim here. The water isn't clean too / enough.
9 He can't wear these shoes. The aren't big too / enough.
10 I don't like this dress. It's too / enough long.

A Activation exercises

Vocabulary: Clothes; Adjectives to describe clothes

1 Complete the descriptions.

This is Julia. She's sixteen years old in this photo. She's wearing ¹ ......*jeans*......, a ² .... and a ³ .... She's got very funny ⁴ .... and ⁵ .... on her feet!

This is William in the garden. In this photo he's wearing a ⁶ ...., a ⁷ .... and ⁸ .... He's got a ⁹ .... on his head.

2 Complete the crossword.

Across

1 It isn't long. It's ....
4 It isn't smart. It's ....

Down

1 It isn't big. It's ....
2 It isn't new. It's ....
3 It isn't old-fashioned. It's ....
5 It isn't tight. It's ....

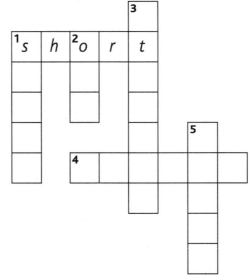

Grammar: *too* + adjective; Adjective + *enough*

3 Write the words in the correct order.

1 film | not | the | enough | exciting | was   *The film was not exciting enough.*...........................

2 are | too | my | for | tight | shoes | me   ....

3 enough | smart | were | clothes | not | her   ....

4 for | this | me | too | weather | cold | is   ....

5 a | casual | party | are | too | for | leggings   ....

6 long | these | jeans | not | enough | are   ....

7 blue | too | the | is | small | shirt   ....

8 enough | not | car | is | his | fast   ....

4 **Match the questions with the answers.**

1 This black T-shirt is too tight.

2 Are these shorts long enough?

3 Do you like those old-fashioned dresses?

4 Can I wear this casual shirt to the concert?

5 Is your belt too small?

a No, they aren't. They're too short.

b No. You need to wear something smart.

c They're pretty but they aren't stylish enough for a party.

d Yes, it is. It isn't big enough.

e Yes, you're right. It isn't baggy enough.

5 **Look at the pictures in Exercise 1 and complete the email with _too_ or _enough_ and the words in brackets.**

My darling Lulu,

Here are some photos for your family photo album – I found them last weekend.

The girl is your mum! She's at a party. She was sixteen in the photo. I think she was pretty but her clothes were awful! Her
¹ _____T-shirt was too baggy_____ (T-shirt / baggy), her
² _____ (jeans / short) and her
³ _____ (shoes / big). And those
socks! ⁴ _____ (she / old) for those
socks! I don't think those ⁵ _____
(clothes / smart) for a party but they were stylish in the 1980s.

I also found this photo of my father. In those days, people usually wore smart clothes in photos but not your great-granddad! His ⁶ _____ (jacket / old)
and his ⁷ _____ (trousers / long)! But he was a gardener and he wore those clothes at work.

See you next weekend.

All my love,
Gran

English today

6 **Complete the dialogue.**

clothes	new	No way!	right	serious	smart enough	~~think~~	too young	wrong

Emma: Hey, everybody! Look at this dress! My friend Fiona gave it to me.
I want to wear it at Grandma's birthday party. What do you ¹ _____think_____?

Luke: Are you ² _____, Emma? You can't wear that!

Emma: Why? What's ³ _____ with it?

Luke: It's too short and too tight! You're ⁴ _____ for dresses like that!

Emma: I'm not! Mum, do you like it?

Mum: Well, I like the colour, Emma, but Luke is ⁵ _____. Why don't you wear your pretty blue dress?

Emma: ⁶ _____ It's old and it isn't ⁷ _____ for a party.
Can you buy me a ⁸ _____ dress, Mum?

Mum: No. You've got lots of ⁹ _____, Emma. You don't need more.

Emma: Oh, Mum!

A Extension exercises

1 **What are they wearing? Write sentences.**

1 Mrs Jones *is wearing a long dress, a big hat with flowers and old-fashioned shoes* .

2 David ....
....

3 James ....
....

4 Lucy ....
....

2 **Match the people in Exercise 1 with the speech bubbles.**

> I hate that photo. I'm wearing my big brother's jacket in that photo. It was too big for me and the trousers were too baggy.

1 .... *James* ....

> I loved those old clothes! They were my mum's, of course. The shoes were too big and the skirt was too long but I thought they were beautiful.

2 ....

> I look terrible! That dress was too long and old-fashioned! My clothes really weren't stylish enough for a wedding!

3 ....

> Wow! I look so young in that photo! But those jeans are awful: too tight and too old. Did we really wear clothes like that in those days?

4 ....

About you

3 **Write sentences. What do you like to wear when you go to ...**

1 a friend's party? ....
2 a school disco? ....
3 the cinema or a concert? ....

Vocabulary: Household jobs

1 **Choose the correct words.**

1 I (make) / do my bed every morning.

2 I load / vacuum my room every weekend.

3 I water / walk the plants in the afternoon.

4 I clear / feed the table after breakfast.

5 I do / make the washing-up at the weekend.

6 I feed / load the dishwasher every day after meals.

7 I make / lay the table every evening.

8 I feed / walk the dog every day.

Grammar: have to

2 **Complete the tables.**

+	
I have to	do jobs at home.
She ¹ ...... *has to*	walk the dog.
–	
I ² .... have to	tidy my brother's room.
She doesn't ³ .... to	do the washing-up.

?	
Do you have to make your bed?	Yes, I do./No, I ⁴ ....
⁵ .... she have to feed the cat?	Yes, she does./No, she ⁶ ....

About you

3 **Answer the questions about you.**

1 Do you have to do jobs at home?   *Yes, I do./No, I don't.* ....

2 Does your friend have to do jobs at home?   ....

3 Do you have to do your homework in the afternoon?   ....

4 Does your mum have to cook dinner in the evening?   ....

5 Does your dad have to go to work by bus?   ....

B Activation exercises

Vocabulary: Household jobs

1 Match the sentence halves.

1 I always do ..*d*..
2 I clear ....
3 I load ....
4 I make ....

5 I never walk ....
6 I sometimes water ....
7 I usually lay ....
8 I often vacuum ....

a my bed every morning.
b the dog.
c the living room on Saturdays.
d the washing-up after breakfast.

e the plants.
f the dishwasher after dinner.
g the table after dinner.
h the table before dinner.

2 Complete the texts.

clear	feeding	load	make	room
~~vacuum~~	washing-up	water		

Household jobs

I hate household jobs! They're the worst thing in the world! Has anybody got any ideas about making them more fun?
Jem

Hey, Jem! This is what I do: I listen to my MP3 player and dance when I ¹ ...*vacuum*... my room.
I also listen to it when I ² .... the plants.
People say plants like music, too! Try it.
SuzieQ

Do household jobs with your brother or sister and have competitions:
• How fast can you ³ .... your bed?
• How quickly can you do the ⁴ ....? (But be careful and don't break the dishes!)
• How quietly can you empty or ⁵ .... the dishwasher?
The winner gets 20p – and I often win!
RickyTicky

Oh, come on, Jem! Some jobs are fun. I enjoy ⁶ .... the dog and walking it. Don't you?
Julia

I think about all the countries I want to visit when I ⁷ .... the table after dinner. Then I find information about them on the Internet.
Pete

I agree with Julia. I like tidying my ⁸ ....!
Am I strange?
ChookieZ

3 Read the texts in Exercise 2 and answer *True* (*T*) or *False* (*F*).

1 SuzieQ sings to her plants. ☐ F
2 SuzieQ dances when she cleans her room. ☐
3 RickyTicky does all his jobs very fast. ☐
4 RickyTicky's brother and sister don't do household jobs. ☐
5 Julia likes some jobs. ☐
6 Pete uses the Internet when he clears the table. ☐
7 ChookieZ doesn't like tidying her room. ☐

Grammar: *have to*

4 Write the words in the correct order.

1 has | empty | to | the dishwasher. | he
He has to empty the dishwasher. ....

2 to | walk | have | every day. | the dog | I
....

3 water | to | don't | we | the plants. | have
....

4 the cats? | have | feed | she | to | does
....

5 in the house. | to | have | they | their parents | help
....

6 you | make | every day? | have | do | your bed | to
....

7 do | to | have | he | doesn't | the washing-up.
....

5 **3 37** Listen to Olivia and Charlie talking to their grandmother and tick (✓) the household jobs they have to do.

	Olivia	Charlie
make the bed		
lay the table		
clear the table		
load the dishwasher		
empty the dishwasher		
feed the dog and the cat		
walk the dog		
walk the cat		

6 Look at Exercise 5 and write sentences about Olivia and Charlie. Use the correct form of *have to*.

1 Olivia and Charlie / make / beds
   Olivia and Charlie have to make their beds.

2 they / lay / the table
   ....

3 they / clear / the table
   ....

4 Charlie / load / the dishwasher
   ....

5 Olivia / empty / the dishwasher
   ....

6 Charlie / feed / the dog and the cat
   ....

7 Olivia / walk / the dog
   ....

8 Olivia and Charlie / walk / the cat
   ....

7 Look at Exercise 5 and write questions and answers about Olivia and Charlie. Use the correct form of *have to*.

1 Charlie / feed / the dog and the cat?
   A: *Does Charlie have to feed the dog and the cat?*
   B: *No, he doesn't.*

2 Olivia and Charlie / lay / the table?
   A: ....
   B: ....

3 they / make / their beds?
   A: ....
   B: ....

4 Olivia / load / the dishwasher?
   A: ....
   B: ....

5 Charlie / walk / the dog?
   A: ....
   B: ....

6 Olivia and Charlie / clear / the table?
   A: ....
   B: ....

B Extension exercises

1 **Read the notes and complete the texts. Use the correct form of *have to*.**

| clear | cook | do | do | feed | load | load | ~~make~~ | tidy | walk | water | water |

Matt, dear, don't forget your household jobs today:

Your bedroom looks terrible. Why are all your computer games in the living room?

Rex needs exercise. He's your dog, remember?

Love, Mum

Matt
Mum works in the shop on Saturdays, and my sister and I have to do the household jobs. First, I ¹ _have to make_ my bed and clean my room. Then I ² .... the living room. Mum's cross because all my games are in there! Finally, I ³ .... the dog. Luckily, I ⁴ .... the plants as well! That's Alice's job!

Alice, darling, please cook breakfast for your brothers but wash things afterwards.

It's hot today, so don't forget the plants. And don't forget Daisy – she looked hungry this morning!

Love, Mum

Alice
Today I ⁵ .... breakfast. After breakfast, I ⁶ .... the table. My little brother, Duncan, ⁷ .... the dishwasher but he ⁸ .... any other jobs. Oh yes! I also ⁹ .... the plants and ¹⁰ .... my cat, Daisy.

Duncan, sweetie, help your sister after breakfast! And do your homework!

Love, Mum

Duncan
I ¹¹ .... the dishwasher after breakfast but then I can go out and play! I love Saturdays! Oh, I forgot! I ¹² .... my homework. Yuck!

2 **Look at Exercise 1 and complete the dialogue.**

Mum: Hi, Alice, I'm home. ¹ *Did you feed the cat?*
Alice: Yes, Mum, I fed the cat.
Mum: ² ....
Alice: Yes, he did. Look, Mum, the living room is tidy!
Mum: ³ ....
Alice: I think so. Rex is sleeping now.
Mum: ⁴ ....
Alice: Yes, he loaded the dishwasher.
Mum: ⁵ ....
Alice: No, he went out to play with his friends.
Mum: No ice cream for Duncan then. And more for us!

About you

3 **Answer the questions about you.**

1 What time do you have to get up in the mornings?
....

2 What time do you have to be at school in the mornings?
....

3 What time do you have to go to bed at night?
....

4 What household jobs do you have to do?
....
....

5 What jobs does your best friend have to do?
....
....

Speaking: Shop for clothes

1 Complete the sentences. Write one word in each gap.

1 Have you got these jeans in a smaller ......*size*......?
2 Can I .... these jeans on?
3 Have you got that shirt in a .... colour?
4 How .... are the shoes?
5 .... T-shirt do you prefer?

2 Put the dialogue in the correct order.

The black skirt looks great. How much is it?	....
And have you also got it in a different colour?	....
Sure, the changing rooms are over there.	....
Excuse me. Have you got this skirt in a smaller size?	*1*
Yes, we have.	....
Can I try the black one on?	....
Yes, we've got it in black and green.	....
Oh! That's too expensive.	*9*
It's £29.99.	....

Your turn

3 Write a dialogue. Use the pictures to help you.

You: *Excuse me.* ....
Assistant: ....
You: ....
Assistant: ....
You: ....
Assistant: ....
You: ....
Assistant: ....
You: ....

Writing: An email about clothes

4 Join the sentences. Use *because* or *so*.

1 I like this T-shirt. It's very stylish.
I like this T-shirt because it's very stylish.
2 These jeans are too long. I can't wear them.
....
3 I'm going shopping. I need some new clothes.
....
4 The dress was very expensive. I didn't buy it.
....
5 He didn't like the trousers. He changed them.
....
6 She didn't wear her new T-shirt. It was too cold.
....
7 Those shirts are cheap. I can buy two.
....
8 I don't want to wear those shoes. They're too old.
....

5 Complete the email with *because* or *so*.

From: valdegal@123email.com
To: lulugregson@123email.com
Subject: Weekend

Hi Lulu,

Thanks for your email. I'm afraid I can't come to the cinema on Sunday. I've got a test on Monday, [1] ......*so*...... I have to study. ☹ And I can't chat to you tonight [2] .... I have to go to town with Mum. We both need some new clothes [3] .... it's my granddad's birthday party on Saturday. He's seventy and he's quite old-fashioned, [4] .... we have to look smart. I can't wear any of my dresses [5] .... they're too short. (That's what granddad says, anyway!) And Mum's favourite dress is too tight for her now, [6] .... she wants to buy a new one. Dad thinks we're silly [7] .... he hates trying on new clothes – he never goes shopping.

Anyway, I have to go now.

See you soon,

Val

Check

1 **Choose the correct answers to complete the dialogue.**

Luke: Hi, Seb. What are you doing?

Seb: Hi, Luke. I'm trying ¹ ..... clothes for Mum and Dad's party tonight. But I can't wear these jeans. They're ² ..... for me.

Luke: What about those trousers?

Seb: They aren't ³ ..... .

Luke: Hmm, you're right. They're ⁴ ..... .

Seb: I'll wear this tracksuit! What do you ⁵ ..... ?

Luke: Are you ⁶ ..... , Seb? You can't wear that!

Seb: Why not? It's a great tracksuit!

Luke: A tracksuit isn't ⁷ ..... for a party. Let's go to town and buy some new clothes.

Seb: Good idea, but I have to come home early. I have to help Mum and Dad with some household jobs.

Luke: What jobs ⁸ ..... to do?

Seb: Well, I have to ⁹ ..... all the rooms and then Mum ¹⁰ ..... vacuum them.

Luke: What about food for the party?

Seb: Dad's making all the food, so Mum ¹¹ ..... cook. And he's a brilliant cook!

Luke: Well, let's go and get some new clothes for the party!

1	**a** on	**b** in	**c** for
2	**a** enough long	**b** tight enough	**c** too baggy
3	**a** enough long	**b** long enough	**c** too long
4	**a** small enough	**b** too short	**c** baggy enough
5	**a** do	**b** know	**c** think
6	**a** wrong	**b** right	**c** serious
7	**a** smart enough	**b** enough smart	**c** enough casual
8	**a** do you have	**b** have you	**c** you have got
9	**a** make	**b** tidy	**c** lay
10	**a** has got	**b** have to	**c** has to
11	**a** doesn't have to	**b** hasn't to	**c** have not to

Score: .... /10

2 **Choose the correct answers.**

1 You can't wear that jacket!
 a What's wrong with it?
 b It's £10.
 c No way!

2 I don't like the yellow T-shirt.
 a The changing rooms are over there.
 b You can change it.
 c How much is it?

3 Which shirt do you prefer?
 a I like it.
 b I don't like it.
 c The blue one.

4 Those shoes are too small for you.
 a Which ones do you prefer?
 b Yes, I need some bigger ones.
 c Yes, they're black.

5 How much is the T-shirt?
 a I'm not sure. Let's ask the assistant.
 b We don't have to buy it.
 c Let's get it.

6 Have you got this dress in a different colour?
 a I want to change it.
 b We've got it in red.
 c I have to wear it.

Score: .... /5

My score is ....!

7 Out and about

A Foundation exercises

Vocabulary: Places of entertainment

1 Write the places of entertainment.

| aquarium | art gallery | bowling alley | funfair | ice rink | museum | safari park | ~~zoo~~ |

  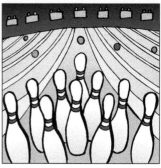 

1 ....zoo....... 2 .... 3 .... 4 ....

5 .... 6 .... 7 .... 8 ....

Grammar: Present continuous for future arrangements

2 Match the questions with the answers.

1 What are you doing on Friday afternoon?
2 Is Julie having a music lesson at four o'clock on Monday?
3 Is Fred meeting his friends at nine on Saturday?
4 Where are Fred and Julie going on Saturday afternoon?
5 Are you going out on Sunday?

a No, she isn't.
b I'm playing tennis.
c Yes, I am.
d Yes, he is. He's meeting them in town.
e They're going to the cinema.

About you

3 Answer the questions about you.

1 Are you going home after school?   *Yes, I am./No, I'm not.* ....
2 Is your best friend playing football this weekend?   ....
3 Are you going to the cinema on Saturday?   ....
4 Is your dad/mum cooking dinner tonight?   ....
5 Are you and your friend meeting this weekend?   ....

A Activation exercises

Vocabulary: Places of entertainment

1 Complete the places of entertainment in the adverts.

1 Welcome to Wessex
A*q u a r i u m*!

Find out all about our amazing sea life!

2 The Wessex
S.......... .... C.......... ....
We've got great activities for everyone. And it's only £10 a month!
• squash • karate • swimming

3 **Come to Wessex Z.......!**
See lions, tigers, elephants, monkeys and hundreds of other animals.

4 Come to the **Wessex Natural History M**.......... ....
and learn all about dinosaurs!

5 The *Wessex*
A.......... ..... *G*.......... ....
This month you can see Francis Jones's beautiful paintings of wild animals.

6 See lions and tigers in the wild – but stay safe in your car!
Visit **Wessex**
S.......... .... P..... ....!

7 Come and enjoy a great time on the ice at the Wessex I......... R...........!
It's free – just pay to hire the skates.

8 With more than fifty shops and fifteen cafés, the **Wessex S**.......... ....
C.......... ....
has something for everyone.

2 Where do they want to go? Match the people with the places of entertainment in Exercise 1.

My mum and I love looking at clothes and shoes, and going to a nice café for lunch.

1 *shopping centre*

My friends and I want to have fun tonight. We want to do something active but the sports centre is too expensive.

2 ....

I like animals but I don't want to go to the zoo. That's for kids! And I don't really like fish.

I don't like art very much but I love learning about history and looking at very old things.

3 ....

4 ....

About you

3 Write about where you want to go. Use Exercises 1 and 2 and these ideas to help you.

- What do you and your friends like?
- What do you want to do?
- Where do you want to go?
- Why do you want to go there?

Grammar: Present continuous for future arrangements

4 Complete the email with the correct verb forms. Use the present continuous.

Hi Granny,

Thanks for your email. What [1] _am I doing_ (I / do) this weekend? Well, I [2] .... (not go) out with my friends because I [3] .... (study) for my exams next week. Yuck! But when the exams finish, my friends and I [4] .... (have) a party.

Dad [5] .... (travel) to Brazil on Monday and he [6] .... (not come) home until Saturday. Lucky him! Mum [7] .... (not go) to work next week. She [8] .... (stay) at home because she wants to paint the kitchen. Boring!

What [9] .... (you / do) next Sunday? Let's do something together when school finishes. How about going bowling?

Lots of love,
Sam

5 **3/38** Listen to Joanna talking to Fred and complete Joanna's diary. Write one or two words in each gap.

Friday
* School visit to the [1] _art gallery_ at 10 a.m.
* 5.00 p.m.: [2] .... lesson
* Evening: family [3] .... with Uncle Pete

Saturday
* Shopping! Meet Marcus and Lucy at [4] .... a.m.
* Meet Mum for lunch at 1 p.m. at Joe's Café in the [5] ....
* Afternoon: visit the [6] ....
* Evening: go to the [7] .... with Lucy and her dad.

6 Look at Exercise 5 and write questions and answers about Joanna.

1 where / Joanna / go / on Friday morning?
A: _Where is Joanna going on Friday morning?_
B: _She's going to the art gallery._

2 she / have / French lesson / on Friday afternoon?
A: ....
B: ....

3 when / she / see / her uncle?
A: ....
B: ....

4 what time / Marcus and Lucy / meet / Joanna on Saturday?
A: ....
B: ....

5 Joanna and her mum / have / lunch / together / on Saturday?
A: ....
B: ....

6 Joanna / go / to the bowling alley with her dad on Saturday?
A: ....
B: ....

7 Put the dialogue in the correct order.

Lucy:	Joanna and I are going to the aquarium on Tuesday afternoon. Why don't you come with us?	....
Marcus:	Oh hi, Lucy.	....
Marcus:	I can't, Lucy. I've got a French exam on Tuesday afternoon.	....
Lucy:	Hi, Marcus. It's me, Lucy.	_1_
Lucy:	Thanks. I'd love to!	....
Marcus:	OK. Call me on Friday afternoon after school. Bye.	_10_
Lucy:	Oh! Bad luck!	....
Marcus:	Well, there's a good film on at the cinema. Would you like to come?	....
Marcus:	Yes, and I'm terrible at French! What about Friday evening? I'm free then.	....
Lucy:	Yes, so am I. What do you want to do?	....

A Extension exercises

1 **Read the dialogue and complete the notes.**

Jenny: So where are we having the surprise party for Emma?

Harriet: At Emma's house.

Jenny: What's a good day for the party?

Harriet: Well, Emma's birthday is on the 16th of May.

Jenny: That's no good. It's a Friday and she's going on a school trip then. What about Saturday?

Harriet: Good idea. Is five o'clock a good time?

Jenny: It's too early. Let's say six o'clock.

Harriet: OK. Now, Ingrid, can you make Emma's birthday cake?

Ingrid: No, sorry, I can't. I'm helping my dad on Saturday morning. Can you make it, Harriet?

Harriet: No! I'm a terrible cook!

Jenny: I can make it. But what about a birthday present?

Harriet: Joe and Ingrid are buying some DVDs for her tomorrow.

Ingrid: What are you doing, Harriet?

Harriet: I'm writing emails to Emma's friends to tell them about the party.

Ingrid: OK. Is there anything else?

SURPRISE PARTY FOR EMMA

- Where? ¹ _Emma's house_
- Date? Saturday ² .... May
- What time? ³ .... p.m.
- Make ⁴ ....: Jenny
- ⁵ .... and ⁶ ....
  : buy present (DVDs!)
- Harriet: send ⁷ .... to
  Emma's friends about party

2 **Read the dialogue in Exercise 1 and answer _True_ (T) or _False_ (F).**

1 Emma's birthday is on 16th May. [T]

2 The party can't be on Friday because Emma's birthday is on Saturday. ☐

3 Five o'clock isn't a good time for the party to start. ☐

4 Ingrid can't make Emma's birthday cake because she's a bad cook. ☐

5 Ingrid can't come to the party because she's helping her dad. ☐

6 Jenny can make cakes. ☐

7 Ingrid and Joe are buying Emma's present on Saturday. ☐

8 Harriet can't go shopping because she has to email Emma. ☐

9 Emma doesn't know about the party. ☐

About you

3 **Answer the questions about you.**

1 What are you doing tomorrow?

....

2 What are you doing next weekend?

....

3 What are your mum and dad doing tomorrow?

....

4 What are they doing next weekend?

....

5 What is your best friend doing on Saturday?

....

6 Are you meeting your best friend tomorrow?

....

7 Is your mum/dad working on Sunday?

....

Memory check: Parts of the body

1 Complete the parts of the body.

1 head

2 e.........................

3 h.........................

4 n.........................

5 a.........................

6 l.........................

7 st.........................

8 f.........................

9 t.........................

10 n.........................

11 sh.........................

12 b.........................

13 f.........................

14 k.........................

Vocabulary: Illnesses

2 Complete the illnesses.

1 fl_u_

2 c.........gh

3 r....nny n...s....

4 t.....th...ch

5 ....r....ch....

6 c....ld

7 st....m....ch ....ch....

8 s...r.... thr.......t

9 h.....d....ch....

10 t....mp....r....t....r....

Grammar: *can* for requests; *can/can't* for permission

3 Choose the correct words.

1 **A:** Can you help me?

   B: Yes, I *can* / *can't*. What do you want me to do?

2 **A:** Can you open the door for me?

   B: No, *sorry*, / *please*, I can't.

3 **A:** Can you come with me to the doctor?

   B: *Yes*, / *No*, of course.

4 **A:** Can you buy me some oranges?

   B: *OK*, / *No*, I can't. I haven't got any money.

5 **A:** Can you give me your dictionary?

   B: *Not now*, / *Of course*, I'm using it.

4 Complete the dialogue with *Yes, you can* or *No, you can't*.

Josh: Mum, can I play in the garden?

Mum: ¹ ....*Yes, you can.*............... (✔)

Josh: Can I go swimming with Sam?

Mum: ² .... (✗)

You've got a cough.

Josh: Can I watch the film on TV tonight?

Mum: ³ .... (✗)

It's on too late.

Josh: Well, can I play a computer game after dinner?

Mum: ⁴ .... (✔), but only

for half an hour.

Josh: Can I use your computer?

Mum: ⁵ .... (✔), but

please be careful with it.

Josh: And can I listen to some music on your MP3

player? Mine isn't working.

Mum: ⁶ .... (✔)

Josh: Thanks, Mum!

B Activation exercises

Memory check: Parts of the body

1 Find and write thirteen parts of the body.

1 ...shoulder...
2 ....
3 ....
4 ....
5 ....
6 ....
7 ....
8 ....
9 ....
10 ....
11 ....
12 ....
13 ....

G	S	H	O	U	L	D	E	R	I	A	W
E	T	O	E	B	A	Q	N	H	A	N	D
F	O	A	Y	J	T	M	K	E	X	E	Z
K	M	E	A	L	E	G	N	A	H	C	Y
B	A	C	K	U	N	I	E	D	A	K	F
A	C	S	A	L	D	O	E	A	A	W	O
J	H	L	C	F	I	N	G	E	R	A	O
D	E	P	N	O	S	E	A	D	M	I	T

Vocabulary: Illnesses

2 Match the speech bubbles with the pictures.

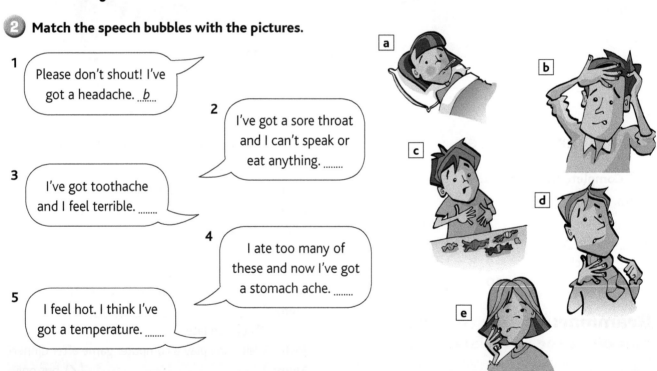

1 Please don't shout! I've got a headache. _b_

2 I've got a sore throat and I can't speak or eat anything. ....

3 I've got toothache and I feel terrible. ....

4 I ate too many of these and now I've got a stomach ache. ....

5 I feel hot. I think I've got a temperature. ....

a
b
c
d
e

Grammar: *can* for requests; *can/can't* for permission

3 Write the words in the correct order.

1 we | can | room? | leave | the   _Can we leave the room?_ ....

2 have | water? | I | a glass of | can   ....

3 your | can | photos? | look at | I   ....

4 parents? | we | can | our | phone   ....

5 you | I | ask | question? | can | a   ....

6 tomorrow? | can | a | picnic | we | have   ....

4 Complete the dialogues. Write one or two words in each gap.

Emma: Luke, [1] _can you_ help me with my homework?

Luke: [2] .... What's the problem?

Emma: I don't understand this exercise. [3] .... do it for me?

Luke: No, I [4] .... This is your homework!

Mum: Luke, [5] .... bring me a cup of tea?

Luke: Yes, [6] .... course, Mum. Do you want anything else?

Mum: Yes, please. Turn off the TV. I've got a headache. Thank you!

Luke: Dad, [7] .... drive me to the cinema?

Dad: [8] .... now, sorry. I'm writing an important email.

Luke: Mum, can you take me?

Mum: No, [9] ...., I [10] .... I'm meeting your aunt Sarah in ten minutes.

5 Write requests.

1 It's very cold. (close / door)
   Can you close the door?

2 You haven't got any money. (give / me / some money / please)
   ....

3 You want your brother to help John. (help / John)
   ....

4 You're thirsty. (bring / me / glass of water / please)
   ....

5 Your sister is talking on the phone but you want to go to sleep. (be / quiet)
   ....

6 Imagine someone asks you the questions in Exercise 5. Answer them.

1 _Yes, of course._
2 ....
3 ....
4 ....
5 ....

7 What are the people saying? Complete the speech bubbles.

Can I have a piece of cake?   ~~Can I open the window?~~   Can we take photos in the museum?
No, you can't.   No, you can't, but you can have an apple.   Yes, of course.
You can listen to your MP3 player but you can't talk.

1 _Can I open the window?_

B Extension exercises

1 Complete the texts. Then match them with the pictures.

| ache | cough | doctor | earache | feeling | ~~ill~~ | matter | miserable | runny | toothache |

What's new?

1

Lily

I'm ¹ _____ill_____ and I'm in bed! The ² _____ says I can't go to school for a week. I'm ³ _____ hot because I've got a temperature. I've also got a sore throat and a terrible headache. What's the ⁴ _____ with me? I've got the flu!

2

Zoe

I went to a great party last night! I danced a lot and I ate a lot, too. In fact, I ate too much cake. I'm really ⁵ _____ today because I've got stomach ⁶ _____. I want to stay at home but my mum says I can't.

3

Alex

I haven't got a ⁷ _____ nose or a ⁸ _____. It's my ears. I've got terrible ⁹ _____, so I'm not going to school. I'm going to the doctor.

4

Sam

I'm not ill but I've got ¹⁰ _____. My mum says I eat too many sweets. And she says I have to go to school.

a ☐ **b** ☐

c ☐ **d** ☐

2 Read the texts in Exercise 1 and write *Lily* (*L*), *Zoe* (*Z*), *Alex* (*A*) or *Sam* (*S*).

Who ...

1 has got a temperature? _L_
2 had a good time last night? _____
3 is going to the doctor? _____
4 is going to school today? _____ and _____
5 ate the wrong things? _____
6 needs to go to the dentist? _____

About you

3 Write a dialogue with your mum or dad about things you want to do. Use these ideas or your own ideas.

- You want to go shopping with your friends on Saturday morning.
- You're tired and you don't want to go to school.
- You want to stay at your friend's house tomorrow.
- You want to watch a horror film on TV at ten o'clock tonight.

You: Can I go shopping with _____?

_____: Yes, of course, but _____

_____.

You: _____

_____

_____: _____

_____

You: _____

_____

_____: _____

You: _____

_____

_____: _____

_____

Vocabulary: Adverbs

1 Complete the table.

Adjective	Adverb
quiet	1 _quietly_
2	correctly
slow	3 ....
fast	4 ....
5	carefully
6	safely
good	7 ....
8	loudly
polite	9 ....

2 Choose the correct words.

1 The road is dangerous. Please drive (carefully) / loudly.
2 You have to talk loudly / politely or I can't hear you.
3 I can play the piano very well / safely. I want to be a professional musician.
4 She answered all the questions safely / correctly and she got an 'A' in the test.
5 Dad is sleeping. Play your music slowly / quietly.
6 Don't run or walk fast! Walk well / slowly.
7 The little boy talked politely / safely to the old lady.
8 His car can go at 240 kilometres an hour. It goes politely / fast!

3 Complete the dialogue with adverbs.

Luke: Emma, please play your music ¹ _quietly_ (quiet) tonight. I have to study for a test.

Emma: I will. I've also got a test tomorrow and I want to answer all the questions ² .... (correct). The last time I made a lot of mistakes.

Luke: That's because you write too ³ .... (fast). You should read the questions ⁴ .... (slow) and then check your answers ⁵ .... (careful).

Emma: Oh! What's that noise?

Luke: Mum and Dad are watching a music programme.

Emma: I'm going to ask them to turn it down.

Luke: Good idea. But ask them ⁶ .... (polite).

Emma: I will, don't worry.

Grammar: Rules with must/ mustn't/can

4 Complete the rules for the camping trip with must (!), mustn't (✗) or can (✓).

Camping trip to France: rules

1 (!) You _must_ bring warm clothes with you.

2 (!) You .... sleep in your tent.

3 (✗) You .... go walking in the woods by yourself.

4 (✓) You .... bring an MP3 player with you.

5 (✗) You .... play loud music!

6 (✓) You .... phone your parents every day.

C Activation exercises

Vocabulary: Adverbs

1 Complete the dialogues with adverbs.

> **Mum:** You're a good guitar player, Dave!
> **Dad:** Yes, you play the guitar really
> ¹ ....._well_......
> **Mum:** But you're too loud.
> **Dave:** No, I'm not. I never play my music
> ² ....
> **Dad:** Your mum's right. You must be quiet. Your sister is studying for an English test.
> **Dave:** Oh, all right. I'll play ³ ....

> **Mum:** Laura, be careful with that knife!
> **Laura:** Don't worry, Mum. I'm cutting the potatoes ⁴ ....
> **Mum:** No, let me cut them. You're too slow.
> **Laura:** Well, I always cut things ⁵ ....
> It's the only safe way!

> **Dad:** Now, Olivia, are these exercises correct?
> **Olivia:** Yes, Dad! I did them all ⁶ ....
> **Dad:** Hmm. You were very fast.
> **Olivia:** I always work ⁷ .... I'm clever!

2 Complete the sentences with adverbs. There can be more than one correct answer.

1 It was a beautiful summer day and they walked to school ....._slowly_......

2 I did my homework slowly and ...., and I didn't make any mistakes.

3 Horses can run very .... – at about fifty kilometres per hour.

4 She answered all the questions .... and she won the first prize.

5 That man over there is talking .... to his friend on his mobile phone.

6 The football team played .... and won the match.

7 The children spoke ....: they said 'please' and 'thank you'.

8 The trip was dangerous but we came home ....

3 Choose the correct answers to complete the email.

> Hi Julie,
>
> I'm back! We arrived home from our holiday two days ago. The trip took us seven hours! Dad drove ¹ .... because Mum hates going fast. She always says: 'Dan, be ² ....! Please drive ³ ....!' I don't know why she says things like that. My dad always drives ⁴ ....
>
> We had a really ⁵ .... holiday but now I'm bored. Mum and Dad want to have a ⁶ .... day at home today because they're still tired after the trip. My brother wants to practise the trumpet but Mum says he can't. Dad's got a headache, and the trumpet is a ⁷ .... instrument.
>
> I must go now. Mum wants me to help her in the kitchen.
>
> See you at school next week!
>
> Harriet

1 **a** slow   **ⓑ** slowly
2 **a** careful   **b** carefully
3 **a** safe   **b** safely
4 **a** good   **b** well
5 **a** good   **b** well
6 **a** quiet   **b** quietly
7 **a** loud   **b** loudly

Grammar: Rules with must/mustn't/can

4 Match the sentence halves.

1 He's travelling to France,   _f_
2 She can use my computer   ......
3 That snake is dangerous, ...
4 You can watch TV   ......
5 The baby is sleeping, ...
6 That's a very expensive watch, ...

a so you mustn't go near it.
b but you mustn't go to bed late.
c so you must talk quietly.
d so you mustn't break it.
e but she must ask me first.
f so he must take his passport with him.

5 Complete the dialogue with *must*, *mustn't* or *can*.

Mum: Luke! Emma! Please come here. I want to talk to you before I go shopping.

Luke: Sure, Mum.

Mum: Now, listen to me. You ¹ _mustn't_ forget to do your household jobs before the weekend. You ² .... make your beds and tidy your rooms. And you ³ .... do your homework today because we're going to the safari park on Sunday.

Emma: OK, Mum!

Mum: Emma, you've got an English test on Monday, so you ⁴ .... study. You ⁵ .... watch TV all day! And Luke, you ⁶ .... forget to feed the cat. You ⁷ .... have some ice cream after lunch but please do the washing up, Emma.

Emma: Of course, Mum.

Luke: Er, Mum, we haven't got any bread for sandwiches.

Mum: Oh! I ⁸ .... buy some from the supermarket.

Luke: And you ⁹ .... phone Granny and tell her about the trip.

Mum: Yes, you're right.

6 Who must do these things? Read the dialogue in Exercise 5 and tick (✓) the correct boxes.

	Luke and Emma	Luke	Emma	Mum
buy bread				✓
do homework				
do the washing-up				
feed the cat				
make beds				
phone Granny				
study for test				
tidy rooms				

7 What do the signs at a safari park mean? Write sentences with *must* and *mustn't*.

feed / animals   touch / animals
leave / safari park before six o'clock
play / loud music   put / rubbish / in bin
ride / motorbikes   ~~stay / in car~~

1

You must stay in your car. ....

2

....

3

....

4

....

5

....

6

....

7

....

C Extension exercises

1 Complete the dialogue. Use *must*, *mustn't* and *can*.

Kim: Hey, Dad! Here's a letter from my teacher, Mrs Thomson. It's about our school trip to France. We're going camping in the Loire Valley.

Dad: What does it say?

Kim: It says [1] *we must be at school at seven o'clock* (we / be / at school / at seven o'clock).

Dad: That means [2] .... (you / wake up / very early).

Kim: Yes, [3] .... (we / be / late) because the bus is leaving at twenty past seven!

Dad: What about clothes?

Kim: Well, [4] .... (we / wear / our own clothes) but Mrs Thomson says [5] .... (we / have / lots of warm clothes) with us – it's often cold in October.

Dad: OK. What else does she say?

Kim: She says [6] .... (we / take / a lot of money) – we don't need much! But [7] .... (we / take / our MP3 players and phones). I'm not taking mine because I don't want to lose them.

Dad: That's great, Kim. Now, remember: [8] .... (you / speak / French) all the time in France and [9] .... (you / behave / politely) at all times.

Kim: Oh, Dad! Why do you say these things?! I always behave well!

2 Read the dialogue in Exercise 1 and answer *True* (*T*), *False* (*F*) or *Don't know* (*DK*).

1 Kim is going to France next weekend. **DK**
2 The bus is leaving for France before half past seven. ☐
3 Kim must wear her school uniform on the trip. ☐
4 The children need warm clothes because it is autumn. ☐
5 Kim isn't taking a lot of money with her. ☐
6 The children mustn't take their MP3 players with them. ☐
7 Kim speaks French very well. ☐

About you

3 Write what you must, can and mustn't do at home.

....
....
....
....
....
....
....
....
....
....

Communication

Speaking: Make requests

1 Complete the dialogues.

ahead	borrow	~~can~~	don't	problem	
suppose	thank	Why?	you		

Seb: Dad, [1] ...... *can* ...... I use your laptop to send an email?

Dad: I [2] .... so, but why don't you use your computer?

Seb: Mum's using it at the moment.

Dad: Oh. Well, [3] .... forget to turn it off when you finish.

Seb: Thanks, Dad.

Luke: Emma, can I [4] .... £5 from you?

Emma: [5] ....

Luke: I can't find my money and I need to buy a mouse for my computer.

Emma: OK. Go [6] .... My money's in my bag. But you must give it back to me next week.

Luke: Thanks, Emma!

Mum: Sophie, can [7] .... make me a cup of tea?

Sophie: No [8] ...., Mum. Are you all right?

Mum: I've got a headache and I think I've got a temperature, too.

Sophie: Well, go to bed and let me bring you your tea there.

Mum: [9] .... you, Sophie.

Your turn

3 You are a member of the Wildlife Club at your school and you want to visit the Longleat Safari Park on 14th June. Write a formal letter to the owner of the park. Use Exercise 2 and these questions to help you.

- What are you writing about?
- When are you arriving?
- When are you leaving?
- How many members are there in your club?
- How old are they?
- Ask the owner what you can see at the safari park.
- Ask if you can take photos of the animals.
- Thank the owner.

Writing: Write a formal letter

2 Put the words in the correct order and write a formal letter.

1 about / to the Wessex Aquarium / I / on 2nd July / our school visit / am / writing

2 and / we / at 2 p.m. / arriving / at 5 p.m. / leaving / are

3 are / the group / in / students / there / forty-two

4 twelve to fourteen / they / years old / are / all

5 a school project / about sharks / they / to learn / want / for

6 information / could you / the different sharks / in the Aquarium / send us / about / please?

7 very / thank / much / you

Dear Mrs Henderson,

[1] *I am writing about our school visit to the Wessex Aquarium on 2nd July.* ....

2 ....

3 ....

4 ....

5 ....

6 ....

7 ....

Yours sincerely,

David Matthews

Dear Sir/Madam,

I am writing ....

....

....

....

....

....

....

....

....

....

....

Yours faithfully,

....

Check

1 **Choose the correct answers to complete the dialogue.**

Seb: Hi, Luke.

Luke: Oh hi, Seb.

Seb: Listen. What [1] .... on Friday afternoon?

Luke: [2] .... to the dentist. I've got [3] ....

Seb: Oh, bad luck! Are you [4] .... on Saturday?

Luke: Yes, I am. Why?

Seb: Well, [5] .... you and Emma like to come to the bowling [6] .... with me and my parents in the afternoon?

Luke: Yes, sure. That sounds fun! But I [7] .... ask my parents first. Emma can't come with us. She's [8] ....

Seb: Oh! I didn't know. What's the matter?

Luke: She's got a [9] .... throat and [10] .... The doctor says she mustn't talk [11] .... and she mustn't go out for a few days.

Seb: I hope she's better soon. Say hi from me.

Luke: OK. See you on Saturday!

1	**a** you are doing	**(b)** are you doing	**c** you do
2	**a** I'm going	**b** I go	**c** I went
3	**a** headache	**b** earache	**c** toothache
4	**a** sure	**b** free	**c** miserable
5	**a** would	**b** can	**c** could
6	**a** rink	**b** gallery	**c** alley
7	**a** can	**b** must	**c** mustn't
8	**a** quiet	**b** ill	**c** slow
9	**a** runny	**b** ache	**c** sore
10	**a** a temperature	**b** a stomach	**c** an ear
11	**a** quiet	**b** loud	**c** loudly

Score: .... /10

2 **Choose the correct answers.**

1 Can you help me with my Science homework?
  a OK, go ahead.
  b You must ask me first.
  (c) Yes, sure.

2 I can't come to the art gallery with you on Friday. I've got a test.
  a Oh, bad luck!
  b OK, go ahead.
  c I suppose so.

3 What are you doing on Thursday evening?
  a Not now, sorry.
  b Would you like to come with me?
  c We're having dinner with our grandparents.

4 I'm not doing anything this weekend.
  a No, sorry, we can't.
  b Why don't you come with us to the bowling alley?
  c OK, you can go.

5 How did he do in the competition?
  a He did well.
  b He did fast.
  c He did carefully.

6 What's the matter with her?
  a No problem.
  b She's feeling miserable.
  c That sounds fun!

Score: .... /5

My score is .... !

8 Happy holidays

A Foundation exercises

Vocabulary: Feelings

1 Complete the words.

1 h_a_pp_y_ **2** b__r__d **3** emb__r__a____ed **4** j__al____s **5** u__s__t

6 n__r____us **7** s____ar__d **8** pr____d **9** ex____t__d **10** a__g__y

Grammar: *going to* for future plans

2 Complete the tables.

+	
I am going to	surf tomorrow.
She [1] _is_ going to	fly to Mexico.
They are [2] .... to	do rock climbing.

–	
I [3] .... not going to	watch TV tonight.
He is [4] .... going to	lie on the beach all day.
We are not going [5]	play football tomorrow.

?	
[6] .... you going to do a film-making course?	Yes, I [7] ..../ No, I'm not.
Is he [8] .... to go to the adventure camp?	Yes, he is./No, he [9] ....

About you

3 Answer the questions about you.

1 Are you going to do your English homework this afternoon?
Yes, I am./No, I'm not.
....

2 Are you going to watch TV tonight?
....

3 Are you going to see your friends this weekend?
....

4 Are you going to stay at home on Sunday?
....

5 Are you going to have a party next month?
....

6 Is your mum going to cook breakfast tomorrow?
....

7 Is your best friend going to call you tonight?
....

8 Are your friends going to play football next week?
....

A Activation exercises

Vocabulary: Feelings

1 Find and write eleven words for feelings.

U	P	S	E	T	P	A	C	M	K	W	O
A	M	S	C	A	R	E	D	R	A	O	B
A	G	A	E	H	O	M	A	F	A	R	O
J	E	A	L	O	U	S	A	A	A	R	R
E	P	A	D	A	D	A	H	A	B	I	E
A	E	M	B	A	R	R	A	S	S	E	D
D	X	O	R	N	A	S	P	G	A	D	A
L	C	B	I	G	A	I	P	M	A	A	L
I	I	A	D	R	E	B	Y	A	F	J	A
A	T	S	F	Y	D	R	I	A	K	A	N
H	E	N	E	R	V	O	U	S	C	A	A
E	D	Y	N	R	A	C	A	H	L	A	F

1 _____upset_____   7 _____
2 _____   8 _____
3 _____   9 _____
4 _____   10 _____
5 _____   11 _____
6 _____

2 Complete the sentences with words from Exercise 1.

1 Yesterday Luke was a _ngry_____ with Emma because she broke his watch.
2 Sophie never feels n_____ before an exam.
3 Emma's parents are p_____ of her because she got the best marks in her class.
4 Seb is e_____ because he's going to go to Brazil next month. He's h_____ because he's going to see his grandparents again.
5 Sophie's parents are w_____ because Sophie is late and she isn't answering her mobile phone.
6 There are no lights in the house and Emma is s_____. She hates the dark.
7 Seb never feels j_____ when his friends get great birthday presents.
8 Emma's mum didn't have enough money to pay in the supermarket and she was e_____.

Grammar: *going to* for future plans

3 Write the words in the correct order.

1 am | spend | I | going | in Rome. | two days | to
I am going to spend two days in Rome.

2 to | for our holidays. | to | we | going | Italy | are | fly
....

3 going | fun | is | at the adventure camp. | have | to | she
....

4 do | on | holiday? | going | he | to | is | rock climbing
....

5 all day? | to | you and your friends | are | on the beach | going | lie
....

6 go | to | are | surfing | going | next week. | they
....

4 Complete the email with the correct verb forms. Use *going to*.

Hi Marta,

It's half-term holiday next week, and my sister Sarah and I [1] ___are going to spend___ (spend) a week at an adventure camp. I can't wait! We [2] _____ (do) rock climbing and lots of other activities. Mum is worried about us because she thinks rock climbing is dangerous. I [3] _____ (learn) to scuba dive and Sarah [4] _____ (learn) to wind-surf. My brothers, Jack and Bob, [5] _____ (stay) at home. Jack [6] _____ (play) football with his friends and Bob [7] _____ (sleep) all day. He's so lazy!

What about you? What are you going to do?

Elsa

5 **3 39** **Listen to David and Nancy talking to their aunt about their holiday plans and tick (✓) the things they are going to do.**

1	go to a summer camp	☐	stay at home	✓
2	swim at the swimming pool	☐	swim in the sea	☐
3	play cricket	☐	play football	☐
4	watch TV	☐	read books	☐
5	visit their grandparents	☐	go out with their friends	☐

6 **Write about David and Nancy. Use Exercise 5 to help you.**

David and Nancy aren't going to go to a summer camp this year. They're ....

....

....

....

....

....

....

....

7 **Write questions and answers about David and Nancy. Use Exercise 5 to help you.**

1 David and Nancy / go / to a summer camp / next week?

A: *Are David and Nancy going to go to a summer camp next week?*

B: *No, they aren't.*

2 they / stay / at home?

A: ....

B: ....

3 where / they / swim?

A: ....

B: ....

4 what sport / they / play?

A: ....

B: ....

5 they / play / cricket?

A: ....

B: ....

6 they / watch / TV?

A: ....

B: ....

7 Nancy / read / any books?

A: ....

B: ....

A Extension exercises

1 **What are they saying? Complete the texts.**

a he's going to go scuba diving	**d** I'm not going to do any sports	**g** we're going to go for rides in the mountains
b I hate those sports	**e** ~~I'm so excited!~~	
c I'm not	**f** I'm so jealous!	**h** What am I going to do?

Ben
¹ _e_ My friend Jimmy and I are going to an amazing summer camp! I'm going to do a film-making course. ² .... because I don't like them. Jimmy loves the water and ³ ....

Toby
⁷ .... My friend Sean is going to go to a great summer camp. It's got wind-surfing, scuba diving and rock climbing. I love rock climbing but my parents want me to go to a really boring camp. I'm going to spend two weeks there and play basketball and football but ⁸ ....

Anjali and Naima
I'm Anjali and this is my sister Naima. We're going to have a lot of fun at summer camp! We're going to take our BMX bikes and ⁴ .... Anjali is going to do rock climbing but ⁵ ....: It's too dangerous for me! ⁶ .... I'm going to go skateboarding.

2 **Match the people in Exercise 1 with the adverts for summer camps. There is one extra advert.**

Hillside Camp
Are you aged 12–16? Do you love sports and outdoor activities? Then Hillside Camp is for you!
- Play football.
- Ride BMX bikes.
- Do rock climbing.
- Go skateboarding.
- Go swimming.

Camp Henry
Have summer fun at Camp Henry! Lots of activities to choose from, including:
- football
- tennis
- basketball
- cricket
- swimming
- dance classes

Happy Camp
Everyone is happy at Happy Camp! There's something exciting for young people aged 12–16! The camp is near a beautiful beach and we've got great water sports. You can enjoy swimming, diving, surfing, scuba diving and wind-surfing.

Seagull Camp
Something for everyone! This beautiful camp is near the beach, so you can go swimming every day. You can also learn scuba diving and wind-surfing. In the evening you can try cookery and film-making classes.

1 ....._Anjali and Naima_..... 2 .... 3 .... 4 ....

About you

3 **Read about the camps in Exercise 2 and choose one for you and your best friend.**

I'm so happy! My friend .... and I are going to ....

....

....

....

B Foundation exercises

Vocabulary: Holiday items

1 Write the holiday items.

| beach mat | camera | flip-flops | guidebook | suitcase | sunglasses |
| ~~sun hat~~ | sunscreen | swimming trunks | swimsuit | towel |

1 *sun hat*

2

3

4

5

6

7

8

9

10

11

Grammar: Possessive adjectives and pronouns

2 Match the possessive adjectives with the possessive pronouns.

1 your   **a** ours
2 my   **b** yours
3 his   **c** theirs
4 our   **d** mine
5 their   **e** hers
6 her   **f** his

3 Choose the correct words.

1 I've got my camera. Have you got *your /* *yours*?
2 This isn't *my / mine* laptop. It's Ben's.
3 Whose tent is this? Is it *their / theirs*?
4 That isn't Jake's phone. It's *her / hers*.
5 Your towels are red and green and *our / ours* are blue and yellow.
6 My guidebook isn't very good. Can I look at *your / yours* guidebook?

B Activation exercises

Vocabulary: Holiday items

1 **Read and write the holiday items.**

1 You wear these to protect your eyes when it's sunny. ....*sunglasses*.............
2 A boy wears these when he goes swimming. ....
3 A girl wears this when she goes swimming. ....
4 You wear these on your feet when you're at the beach. ....
5 You need this to read about places when you go on holiday. ....
6 You put all your things in this when you go on holiday. ....
7 You use this to take photos. ....
8 You put this on your skin to protect it from the sun. ....
9 You use this when you get out of the sea or out of the bath. ....
10 You wear this on your head when it's sunny. ....

2 **This family is going on holiday. Match the lists with the suitcases.**

1 ..c..

Mary and Greg
*camera ✔
*guidebook ☐
*sun hat ☐
*sunscreen!! ☐
*sunglasses ☐
*swimming trunks ☐
*towels ☐

a

2 ....

Andrew
. beach mat ☐
. camera ☐
. flip-flops ☐
. sunglasses ☐
. swimming trunks ☐
. towel ☐

b

3 ....

Suzie
* beach mat ☐
* flip-flops ☐
* sun hat ☐
* sunscreen ☐
* sunglasses ☐
* swimsuit ☐

c

VISIT ITALY

DAD MUM

3 **Read the lists in Exercise 2 and tick (✓) the things you can see in each suitcase.**

Grammar: Possessive adjectives and pronouns

4 Choose the correct words.

1 **A:** Whose camera is this?
  B: It's (my) / mine camera.

2 **A:** Whose flip-flops are those?
  B: They're her / hers.

3 **A:** Whose tent is it?
  B: It's their / theirs tent.

4 **A:** Whose sunscreen is it?
  B: It's your / yours.

5 **A:** Whose towels are these?
  B: They're our / ours.

6 **A:** Whose hiking boots are they?
  B: They're my / mine.

7 **A:** Whose guidebook is this?
  B: It's our / ours guidebook.

8 **A:** Whose sunglasses are these?
  B: They're your / yours sunglasses!

5 Look at the pictures in Exercise 2 and complete the dialogues with possessive adjectives or pronouns.

1 **Suzie:** The swimming trunks with the cars on them are funny! Whose are they?
  Andrew: They're ___mine___!

2 **Andrew:** Whose guidebook is *Visit Italy*? Is it Mum and Dad's?
  Suzie: Yes, it's _____.

3 **Suzie:** Is this white towel Mum's?
  Andrew: No, it isn't _____ towel. _____ has got the word 'Mum' on it. That's my towel.

4 **Andrew:** Whose is the big sun hat? Is it _____?
  Suzie: No, _____'s got flowers on it. That one's Mum's.

5 **Suzie:** Is this camera Dad's?
  Andrew: No, _____ is big. That's _____ camera.

6 **Andrew:** Whose flip-flops are these?
  Suzie: They're _____, silly! They're in your suitcase!

7 **Andrew:** Where's Mum? I've got _____ sunglasses here.
  Suzie: No, those aren't _____ – they're _____. Mum's sunglasses are white.

6 Choose the correct answers to complete the email.

Hi Anna,

We're going to go to Italy for our holiday this year! I packed [1] _____ suitcase last night and everything's ready. Well, [2] _____'s ready but Andrew says he's going to pack [3] _____ things tomorrow. Mum and I have got new swimsuits. [4] _____ is blue and [5] _____'s white with flowers on it. Andrew and I have also got new beach mats. Mum and Dad haven't. [6] _____ are old and [7] _____ suitcase is very old, too! My beach mat is so cute! It's got cats on it. I don't like Andrew's beach mat. [8] _____ has got aliens on it. I think it's silly but he loves it.

Where are you going to go for [9] _____ holiday? I bet [10] _____ is going to be more fun than [11] _____!

Suzie

1	**(a)** my	**b** mine	**c** theirs
2	**a** my	**b** mine	**c** our
3	**a** he	**b** his	**c** her
4	**a** She	**b** Her	**c** Hers
5	**a** your	**b** mine	**c** yours
6	**a** Theirs	**b** His	**c** Hers
7	**a** their	**b** theirs	**c** them
8	**a** Her	**b** His	**c** Their
9	**a** ours	**b** mine	**c** your
10	**a** ours	**b** our	**c** my
11	**a** her	**b** your	**c** yours

English today

7 Put the dialogue in the correct order.

Do me a favour. My suitcase is smaller than yours. Can you take my computer games and hiking boots? ....

The clothes on the bed are mine. I'm going to pack them in my suitcase. ....

Whose things are these in the bag? ___1___

And what about all those clothes on the bed? ....

Do you need all those clothes? ....

The blue bag? I'm not sure. I think they're Mum's. ....

You're joking! Pack them in your suitcase or leave them at home! ___9___

Yes, I do. Er ... Andrew? ....

What is it? ....

B Extension exercises

① **Complete the texts. There are two extra sentences.**

a	Hers are boring!
b	I think ours are better.
c	Mine is pink and his is red!
d	Please tell me yours!
e	She put them in mine!
f	Theirs is bigger!
g	Yours is yellow.

Jake	My sisters Anna and Kate always take too many things with them on holiday. Last year Anna didn't pack her swimsuit, flip-flops and beach mat in her suitcase. [1] _e_
Ollie007	Hey, dude! I had the same problem last year. Then I told my sisters: 'This is my suitcase, not yours. Why don't you put your things in Mum and Dad's suitcase? [2] ____ '
DizyLizzie	My brother always uses my towel when we go to the beach, and I hate that! He says our towels look the same but that isn't true. [3] ____ My brother is silly sometimes!
Sara347	We spend our holidays in a different place every year. I've got great ideas about where to go but my parents don't listen to them. They only listen to my sister's ideas. I don't understand it. Mine are brilliant! [4] ____
Zilla	Hey, Sara347! I've got some good ideas, too. [5] ____! Then we can compare them!

② **Read Jake's questions and Ollie's notes and complete Ollie's email.**

1 Where are you going on holiday this year?
2 Who are you going with?
3 Are you going to pack a big or a small suitcase?
4 What things are you going to take with you?
5 What activities are you going to do?

- Spain — two weeks in August!
- Mum, Dad — and my cousin Alfie is coming with us
- big suitcase!
- camera, sunglasses, sunscreen, swimming trunks — and my computer games and games console!
- swimming, scuba diving and rock-climbing

To: Jake
From: Ollie

Hi Jake,
Thanks for your questions!
1 _I'm going to Spain for two weeks in August._
2 _____
3 _____
4 _____
5 _____
Ollie

About you

③ **Answer the questions about you.**

1 Do you go to the same place on holiday every year?

....

2 Where do you go?

....

3 What things do you take with you?

....
....

4 What do your mum or dad take with them on holiday?

....
....

Speaking: Talk about holiday plans

1 Write the words in the correct order.

1 take | Mum and Dad | to | going | on | are | holiday. | us

Mum and Dad are going to take us on holiday.

2 leave? | when | to | are | going | you

....

3 you | going | to | are | go? | where

....

4 great | time! | have | a

....

5 there? | you | what | going | to | are | do

....

6 where | stay? | to | are | you | going

....

2 Complete the dialogue with the sentences in Exercise 1.

Sophie: Hi Luke! You look happy.

Luke: Yes, [1] *Mum and Dad are going to take us on holiday.*

Sophie: Lucky you! When?

Luke: Next week some time.

Sophie: [2] ....

Luke: The Yorkshire Dales.

Sophie: [3] ....

Luke: With a friend of Mum's.

Sophie: [4] ....

Luke: We're going to go hiking and horse-riding.

Sophie: Oh! I'm so jealous! Seb's also going to go on holiday.

Luke: What about you?

Sophie: We aren't going to go anywhere.

[5] ....

Luke: Next Monday, I think.

Sophie: [6] ....

Writing: Write about your plans

3 Read Nina's letter and put the paragraphs in the correct order.

1 how she's going to travel ....c....

2 where she's going to stay ....

3 what she's going to do there ....

4 how she feels ....

Hi Sam,

a We're going to spend two weeks at a summer camp in Majorca. We're going to stay at a campsite and sleep in the same tent.

b I'm so happy and excited, and all my friends are jealous! Mum and Dad are worried about me but everything will be great!

c Guess what! I'm going to go to Spain next week! I'm going to fly to Majorca and my friend Maria is going to meet me at the airport.

d The campsite is near the beach, so we're going to go swimming every day. We're also going to learn scuba diving and wind-surfing.

Lots of love,
Nina

Your turn

4 Imagine you are Sam. Write a letter to Nina about your holiday plans. Use Exercise 3 and these ideas to help you.

- Where are you going to spend your holiday?
- How are you going to get there?
- Who are you going to go with?
- Where are you going to stay? (Is it a hotel, a holiday camp, a friend's house?)
- What activities you going to do?

Check

1 **Choose the correct answers to complete Rob's blog.**

Summer fun!

I can't wait for this summer! I ^{1} .... going to spend two weeks in Europe! The idea for the holiday wasn't ^{2} .... It was my ^{3} .... His best friend, Helmuth, is German, and he and his family ^{4} .... going to come to England and spend two weeks with us in July. Then we're ^{5} .... to go to Germany. Helmuth is going to ^{6} .... us around Germany. And then we're going to go camping, rock-climbing and mountain biking!

My friend Max ^{7} .... going anywhere. He's ^{8} .... because he wants to come with me but he can't. He's going to ^{9} .... at home. My cousin Jenny is going to go to Sardinia. She wants to lie in the sun all day on her beach ^{10} .... I think our holiday is more exiting than ^{11} .... What do you think?

Rob

1	**(a)** 'm	**b** 's	**c** 're
2	**a** her	**b** our	**c** mine
3	**a** dad	**b** dad's	**c** dads
4	**a** am	**b** is	**c** are
5	**a** going	**b** go	**c** goes
6	**a** drive	**b** drives	**c** driving

7	**a** am not	**b** isn't	**c** is
8	**a** scared	**b** jealous	**c** embarrassed
9	**a** spend	**b** see	**c** stay
10	**a** mat	**b** screen	**c** trunks
11	**a** your	**b** my	**c** hers

Score: .... /10

2 **Choose the correct answers.**

1 Whose swimming trunks are those?
  (a) They're John's.
  b They're Mary's.
  c He's bored.

2 Where are you going to go?
  a With a friend.
  b Tomorrow.
  c To Devon.

3 How do you feel?
  a I'm excited!
  b It's scary.
  c They're ours.

4 Why are you upset?
  a Because I haven't got anything to do.
  b Because I can't go on holiday this year.
  c Because it's my birthday today.

5 What are you going to take with you to the beach?
  a A suitcase for the sun.
  b Some sunscreen. It's hot today.
  c It's exotic.

6 Whose towel is that?
  a I'm not sure.
  b It's for the beach.
  c What is it?

Score: .... /5

My score is ....!